THE HISTORY AND TECHNIQUES
OF THE GREAT MASTERS

RUBENS

THE HISTORY AND TECHNIQUES
OF THE GREAT MASTERS

RUBENS

Andrew Morrall

CHARTWELL
BOOKS, INC.

A QUARTO BOOK

Published by Chartwell Books
A Division of Book Sales, Inc.
110 Enterprise Avenue
Secaucus, New Jersey 07094

ISBN 1-55521-263-8

This book was designed and produced by
Quarto Publishing plc
The Old Brewery, 6 Blundell Street
London N7 9BH

Project Editor Hazel Harrison
Designer Terry Smith
Picture Researcher Carina Dvorak

Art Director Moira Clinch
Editorial Director Carolyn King

Typeset by QV Typesetting Ltd
Manufactured in Hong Kong by Regent
Publishing Services Limited
Printed in Hong Kong by Leefung-Asco
Printers Ltd

Contents

Introduction
— 6 —

Chronology
— 20 —

The Paintings

The Judgement of Paris
— 22 —

The Artist and his Wife in a Honeysuckle Bower
— 26 —

Samson and Delilah
— 30 —

The Descent from the Cross
— 34 —

Lion Hunt
— 38 —

The Arrival of Marie De' Medici at Marseilles
— 42 —

The Duke of Buckingham Conducted to the Temple of Virtus
— 46 —

Allegory of Peace and War
— 50 —

The Rape of the Sabine Women
— 54 —

Autumn Landscape with a View of Het Steen
— 58 —

Index
— 62 —

Acknowledgements
— 64 —

INTRODUCTION

PETER PAUL RUBENS
Self-portrait (detail)
c1639
Kunsthistorisches Museum,
Vienna

The life and work of Peter Paul Rubens embody the character and qualities of his age. He seems to have been entirely in harmony with the values and aspirations of his society, and his protean talents, which were to make him as much diplomat as painter and give him the ear of the most powerful figures in Europe, afforded him a position of significance as much on the stage of world affairs as in the history of art. In this sense his career seems, more than that of other great seventeenth-century artists, to be intimately linked to the central political and cultural issues of his time.

Social and political background
Rubens was born into a Europe which, although rent by religious discord, witnessed within the Catholic nations a tremendous upsurge of spiritual confidence accompanied by a period of great wealth for the papacy. Beginning in Rome, vast rebuilding and refurbishing programs were begun, encouraged by new evangelizing orders such as the Jesuits, which spread to all parts of Europe and far beyond. Gradually a new kind of religious imagery emerged that expressed this buoyant, zealous mood. As laid down as early as 1563 at the Council of Trent, the purpose of religious images was both to instruct and to involve the laity emotionally. The hallmarks of the new style were accordingly legibility, realism, and a concern with moving, dramatic and spiritually uplifting themes.

The seventeenth century also witnessed the emergence of absolute monarchies: Louis XIV in France, Charles I in England and Philip IV in Spain; and the rhetorical, emotional and overblown idiom that was developed to extol the Martyrdom of the Saints was recognized as equally appropriate in celebrating the Divine Right of Kings. Rubens played a central role in the creation of this style. As a devout Catholic who celebrated Mass every day he could paint with total conviction the monumental decorations for the Jesuit church in Antwerp; as courtier and diplomat he could paint with equal facility the grand ceiling of the Banqueting Hall in Whitehall, glorifying the reign of James I. His art becomes the expression of a precise historical moment; even the contradictions of his art are those of the age, as for example the overt and enthusiastic sensuality that went hand in hand with a sincere piety.

The first decades of the century, when Rubens came of age as an artist, were a time of positive and creative reaction to the styles of the preceding century. These, with a few great exceptions, had degenerated into a highly stylized, anti-naturalistic aestheticism in which elegant and attenuated forms were favored at the expense of content or expressive value — the style known today as Mannerism. Like other great artists of the day, Bernini and Caravaggio in Rome, Velazquez in Spain and Rembrandt in nearby Holland, Rubens broke with this tradition — in which he was initially trained — by means of a direct and fresh study of nature, modified in his case by a deep immersion in the art of antiquity and that of the High Renaissance. By education and temperament he was the natural heir to the Humanist classical tradition. Throughout his life he possessed a love of classical literature and thought that was to mold his whole outlook on life and determine the classical bias of his art. Stylistically he absorbed certain tenets of classical and High Renaissance art, namely a sense of monumentality and idealization of form; an idea of the clear relationship of the parts to the whole; and the grand tradition of *"disegno,"* the poised and balanced grouping of figures within a harmonious whole. Rubens' particular greatness lies in developing and extending these principles of style in conformity with the tastes and passions of his own day. His monumental works for Church and court alike sanctioned the pretension of his patrons by tying them to history and to tradition through stylistic and iconographical reference to the Renaissance and to the antique.

Early life

The circumstances of Rubens' birth demonstrate the religious uncertainty of the times. He was born on June 28, 1577, at Siegen in Westphalia, and spent the first ten years of his life in Cologne. His father Jan was a native of Antwerp, where he had been a respected lawyer and city alderman until he fell prey to the religious struggles of the time. As both part of the hereditary Catholic Spanish Empire and a continuing center of the Protestant Reformation, the Low Countries became engulfed in religious conflict after the death of the moderate emperor Charles V. Charles's son Philip II of Spain, championing a rigid Catholic orthodoxy, precipitated the opposition of the Flemish nobles, led by William of Orange-Nassau. They actively espoused the Protestant cause in their attempt to gain political and religious freedom. This led, in 1568, to a long and burdensome war, concluded only in 1648, but which resulted more immediately in the separation of the northern, Protestant, United Provinces from Catholic, Spanish, Flanders.

Originally a Catholic, Jan Rubens converted to Protestantism following the changing political and religious sympathies of Antwerp, only to hastily reconvert when the Spanish brought the city to heel in 1567. The following year he left the city together with his family and settled in Cologne, where he became legal advisor to Anne of Saxony, who had been left behind by her husband William of Orange in his struggle against the Spanish. In the course of his duties Jan unfortunately succeeded in getting his employer pregnant and was duly condemned to death for adultery. He was saved only by the magnanimity of his wife, who pleaded unceasingly for clemency. Though spared, and allowed eventually to live with his family, Jan was placed under

JOACHIM WTEWAEL
The Judgement of Paris
1615
National Gallery, London

This work, although painted fifteen years later than Rubens' version (see page 23), shows a typically Northern Mannerist treatment of an Italianate subject. This is evident in the profusion of meticulously painted details, subsidiary figures and animals as well as in the harsh lighting and palette. The elegant insouciance of the poses shows the artist's concern for decorative sophistication at the expense of narrative power.

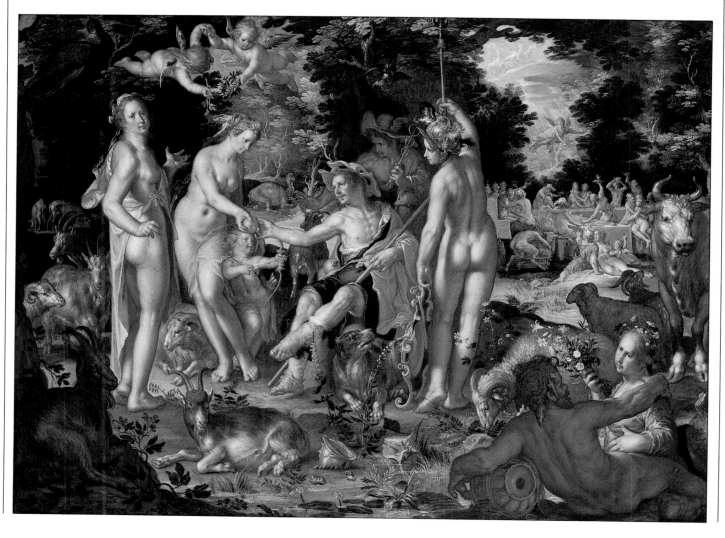

virtual house arrest in Siegen. There, with the resumption of normal family life, his wife gave birth to first Philip in 1576, then Peter Paul in 1577, followed by a sister in 1578. Only in that year was the family fully released and allowed to live anywhere except within the lands of Nassau. They moved back to Cologne and returned to the Catholic faith. Such was the capricious play of circumstances that made Peter Paul Rubens a Catholic and gave the Counter-Reformation one of its greatest propagandists.

Ten years later, on Jan's death, the family moved back to Antwerp, now permanently part of the Spanish Empire and Catholic in its allegiance. Though undergoing a steep economic decline, accelerated by the Dutch blockade of the mouth of the river Scheldt, which prevented access to its port, the city nonetheless continued to possess considerable financial and cultural resources. It became a focus of the Counter-Reformation in the north and witnessed a massive campaign of restoration of its churches, damaged or destroyed in the successive waves of iconoclasm that had swept over the city.

Rubens received a liberal classical education at a school run by a man named Rombout Verdonck. A love of classical literature, bred here and encouraged by his scholarly elder brother, bore fruit in a lifelong passion for the classical past. Through his brother, he was influenced by the Stoic philosophers, in particular Seneca and Plutarch, who advocated seriousness, moderation in all things, the pursuit of virtue, a belief in reason over the passions and an acceptance of fate. Such values were to become the guiding principles of his life.

Artistic training

After serving briefly as a page in the service of Margaret de Ligne-Arenberg at Oudenarde, he entered, in about 1592, the studio of the landscapist Tobias Verhaecht, thereafter moving to that of Adam van Noort, who specialized in portraits. Here he stayed for four years of apprenticeship, and in about 1596 he moved to the studio of Otto van Veen, the most prestigious painter in Antwerp at the time. This master had traveled to Rome and thus knew at firsthand the works of antiquity and of the Renaissance. Like his pupil he was interested in classical literature and, according to Humanist custom, had latinized his name to Octavius Vaenius. From him Rubens learned something of the principles of Renaissace figurative painting, and from his years of apprenticeship in general he learned the methods, techniques and palette of late Mannerist Flemish painting. By 1598 he had enrolled in the Guild of St Luke and had probably set up as an independent painter. Very few works have survived from this period, but the *Judgement of Paris* (see page 23), painted about 1600, shows the characteristics of his early style. The smooth, enamel-like flesh modeling and the palette of acid and discordant colors are entirely northern in conception, comparable to Joachim Wtewael's painting of the same theme. The figural composition however, is derived from Italian prints, in particular Marcantonio Raimondi's engraving after Raphael's treatment of the same subject (see page 23). This well illustrates the chief means by which Rubens came into contact with the Italian tradition. Other sources that are known to have been available to him include the great northern graphic masters. He copied Dürer prints as well as Holbein's *Dance of Death* woodcuts, and thus absorbed certain northern characteristics,

PETER PAUL RUBENS
Ignudo (after Michelangelo)
c 1601-2
British Museum, London

Drawings of this type show how fast Rubens began to absorb the Italian Renaissance tradition. He shows the traits characteristic of Northern

artists — the reluctance to generalize forms, the exact delineation of musculature and the specific, individual physiognomy that he gives the head. The violent torsions of Michelangelo's figures were important in forming the basis of Rubens' dynamic compositions.

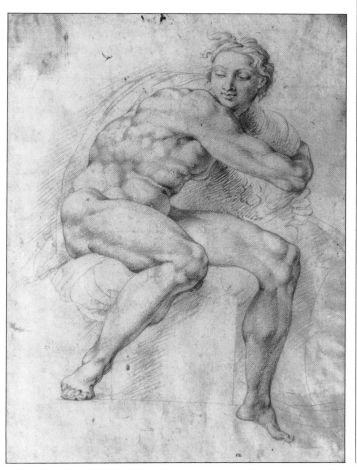

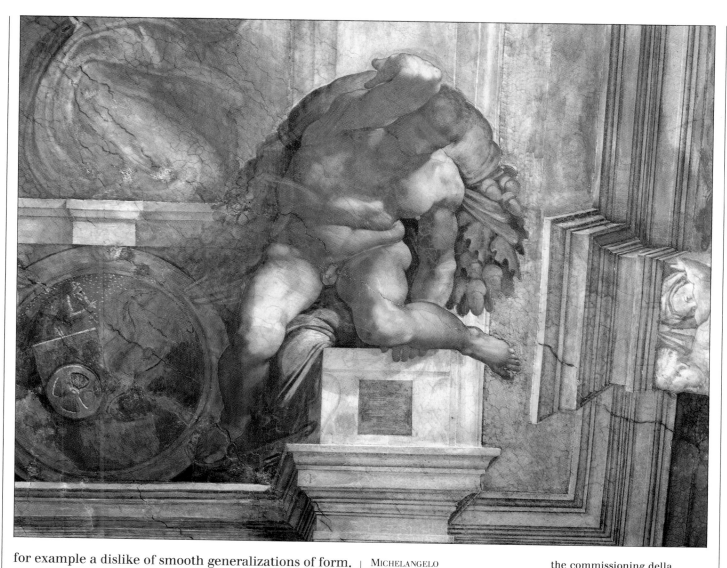

for example a dislike of smooth generalizations of form.

The *Judgement of Paris* was probably completed shortly before his departure for Italy in May 1600. With his apprenticeship finished, Rubens clearly felt that his education would remain incomplete until he had studied the art of Italy at firsthand. Like two other great northern artists of his century, Claude Lorraine and Nicolas Poussin, he felt the tug of the south, sensing the pull of a cultural and artistic tradition which he knew only incompletely. Once in Italy, he immediately recognized it as his spiritual home, leaving it only with great reluctance and with a lifelong desire to return, though this was to be denied him.

The court painter

Traveling initially to Venice, he soon found a position as a court painter to Vincenzo I Gonzaga, Duke of Mantua, and remained thus employed for the next seven years. His duties in Mantua were light, owing to the exiguous state of the duke's finances, and Rubens was therefore free to travel and to find commissions elsewhere. He was

MICHELANGELO
Ignudo, detail of the Sistine Chapel ceiling

This is one of the idealized male nudes that flank the scenes of the Creation. They carry swags of oak leaves and acorns, the family insignia of the commissioning della Rovere pope, Julius II, but their further iconographical significance is unclear. Their elegant, serpentine poses were greatly admired by sixteenth-century artists and continuously emulated in succeeding centuries.

in Rome by July 1601, after already having witnessed the proxy marriage of Marie de' Medici to Henry IV of France in Florence in October 1600.

During the following years Rubens was to travel widely in Italy and to paint some forty works. Many more sketches and drawings survive from this period. A very large proportion of these were copies of things he had seen, and it is clear from their variety and number that he was quite deliberately forming a kind of personal reference library for his future use. That this was to be a fundamental part of his working process can be illustrated vividly by a copy of one of the *Ignudi* of Michelangelo's Sistine Chapel ceiling, made soon after his

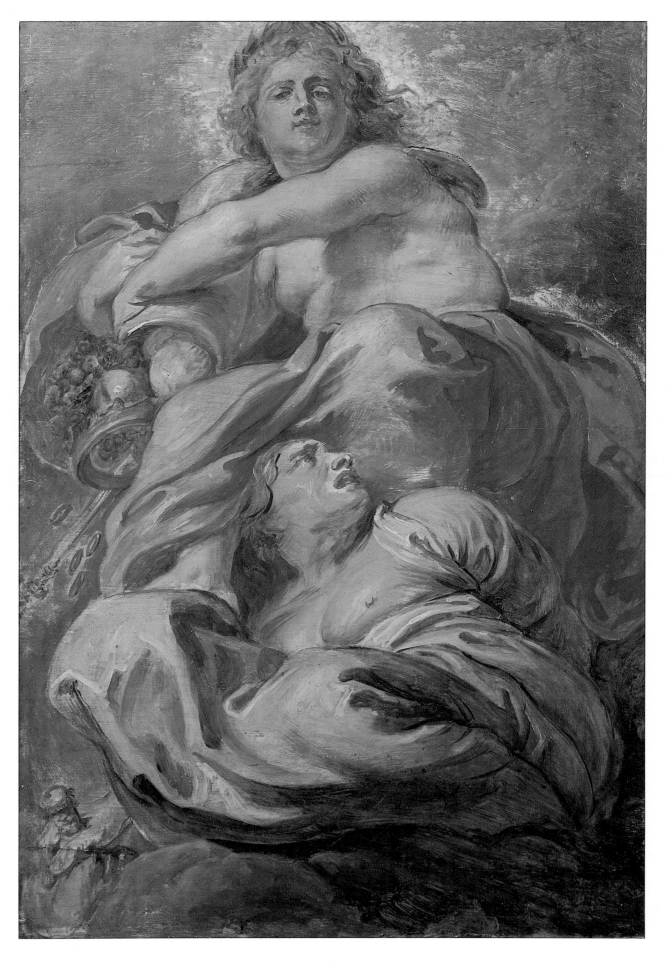

arrival in Rome. He has exaggerated the musculature and made the expression of the face more specific, thus losing the "spiritual" aestheticism of the original. That he kept this drawing and put it to later use is made clear by the existence of a counter-proof of the drawing with the figure extensively reworked that was used in the 1630s as a study for the figure of Bounty in the ceiling decorations of the Banqueting Hall in Whitehall, London. An oil-sketch for the same figure shows the same pose in reverse, now female and partially draped, the bend of the torso made less acute and the angle of vision more steeply foreshortened.

He also copied the most famous antique statues in the Roman collections, including the *Laocoön* group and the so-called "Belvedere torso." He made studies after Titian and Raphael as well as a host of other sixteenth-century artists as diverse as Tintoretto, Cigoli and Barocci. Rubens was also deeply interested in contemporary artistic developments. No sources exist that would prove that he was personally acquainted with Caravaggio, yet it was Rubens who persuaded the Duke of Mantua to buy Caravaggio's controversial *Death of the Virgin* altarpiece when the original commissioners rejected it on grounds of decorum. Variations he made on Caravaggio's *Entombment* demonstrate his interest in his contemporary and show the characteristic manner in which, although drawing inspiration for his own work from that of others, he could completely transform the original into a personal statement. Here he has increased the number of figures, widened the sense of space and unified the group by subordinating them to a single, generalized rhythmic flow of movement.

PETER PAUL RUBENS
Sketch for *Royal Bounty Overcoming Avarice*
c 1632-3
Courtauld Institute Galleries, London

Echoes of Michelangelo's *Ignudo* can be found in several of Rubens' compositions, but these are perhaps clearest in the figure of Bounty, destined for the ceiling of the Banqueting Hall, London, in praise of the unification of Scotland and England under James I. The figure has been reversed by taking a counterproof of the original drawing, and the oak-leaf swags of the original have been transformed into an overflowing cornucopia.

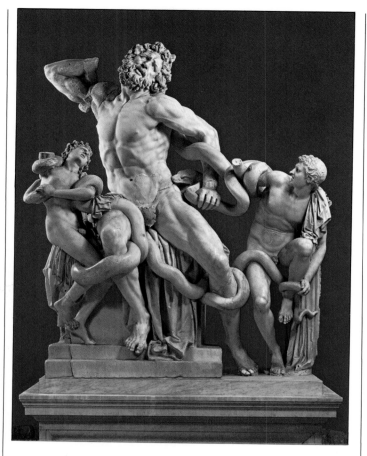

Laocoön
Second century BC
The Vatican, Rome

This famous late-Hellenic sculpture, excavated in 1506, was one of the major discoveries of the Italian Renaissance, and in its monumentality of form and pathos of mood it became a source of inspiration to many painters and sculptors. The subject is a Trojan priest and his sons being devoured by snakes after having warned the citizens of Troy not to bring the Greeks' wooden horse into the city.

Most great artists have drawn frequently on the art of the past for inspiration, but Rubens was exceptional in that, throughout his life, this habit was an almost necessary precondition for creation. He seems to have relied on study of other works of art in order to prompt formal ideas of his own. He was criticized for this even in his own day, but as Roger de Piles, the French seventeenth-century critic, sympathetically put it, he used "all that was most beautiful to stimulate his humor and warm his genius."

In 1603 the Duke of Mantua sent Rubens on a diplomatic mission to King Philip III of Spain, which was to initiate a highly successful career as a diplomat. He performed all his required duties, even restoring and in some cases repainting pictures that had been intended as gifts and which had been damaged en route. In Spain Rubens had the opportunity to study the great royal col-

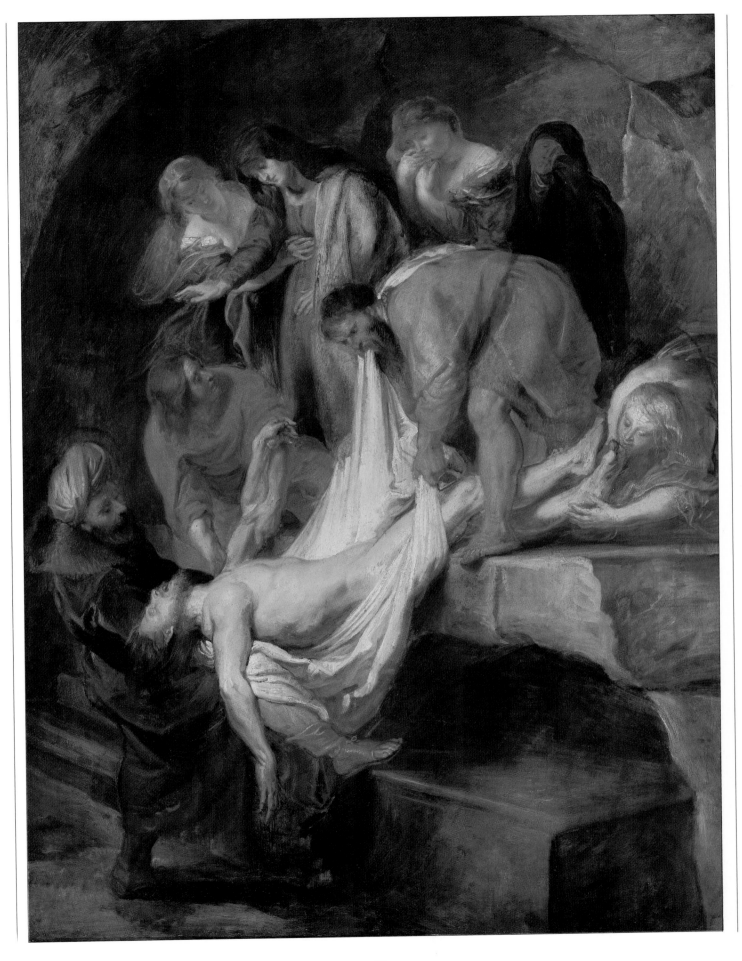

lection, and was particularly impressed by the number and richness of the Titians and Raphaels. By the end of his period away from home, he had had ample opportunity to study the greatest works of art in Europe. His style in this decade was eclectic and experimental; through intense study he broadened his technique, increased his facility with the paintbrush, widened his vocabulary of gesture, posture and expression and learned to paint on a large scale.

Rubens abruptly left the service of the Duke of Mantua in 1608, returning hurriedly to Antwerp upon hearing that his mother was very ill (she had in fact died even before the message reached him). He came back to his home town preceded by a considerable reputation, and quickly established himself as the leading painter of the city. He was commissioned by the city authorities to paint a large *Adoration of the Kings* for the chamber of state, and within a year of his return became court painter to the Regents of the Netherlands, the liberal Archduke Albert of Austria and his wife, Isabella, daughter of Philip II of Spain. He entered their service reluctantly, "bound," as he said, "with fetters of gold" to the tedious injunctions of court life. Yet the privileges that the position conferred were considerable. He was allowed to work in Antwerp (not at the court in Brussels), was exempted from guild regulations and dues and was given an annuity of 500 florins. Moreover, his duties at court were fairly light, consisting mainly of routine portrait painting.

Marriage and prosperity

In addition he married. His wife was Isabella Brant, the eighteen-year-old daughter of a secretary of the city and respected member of the burgher class. The double portrait that he executed as a memento of the wedding (see

PETER PAUL RUBENS
The Entombment
c 1616-18
Courtauld Institute Galleries,
London

This oil-sketch illustrates the way in which Rubens developed the formal ideas of another painting into a personal creation of his own. He has retained the basic colors of Caravaggio's original as well as the protruding corner of the stone slab that seems to invade the spectator's space. Yet the figures are arranged dynamically within an overall shape, echoed by the curves of the cave roof.

page 27) is interesting both as an example of his portraiture style in 1610 and as a revelation of how he saw himself, or how he wished himself to be seen — not as an artist but as a worldly and prosperous gentleman. He is elegantly dressed with ruff and jeweled sword, and sits in a pose of easy assurance, gallantly deferring to his wife, who clasps his hand with shy and unaccustomed intentness.

In November 1610 he began building a large and imposing house which also afforded plenty of studio space for his growing workshop. This house he gradually filled with art and antiques. He had begun to collect

CARAVAGGIO
The Entombment
1602-4
The Vatican, Rome

This painting for a chapel in Rome shows Caravaggio's sharp, descriptive realism, dramatic lighting and use of "peasant types" to represent holy personages, all of which created a new tradition in painting in the early

seventeenth century. Caravaggio's works were regarded as profane by many of the clergy and populace, and initially found favor only among a small circle of wealthy connoisseurs. Rubens immediately recognized his genius, and he made a copy of this work, subsequently elaborating it into a larger composition.

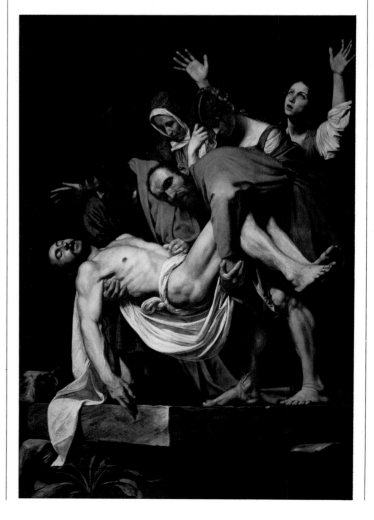

antique statuary while still in Italy, but the greater part of his collection was acquired in a transaction with Sir Dudley Carleton, an English diplomat, who between 1618 and 1620 exchanged some 129 pieces of classical sculpture and marble for six large paintings by Rubens. The result was the best collection of classical remains in northern Europe, and it became one of the sights for visitors to Antwerp.

Yet quite apart from the prestige value of such a collection, it is clear that sculpture was an important source of inspiration for his own work. Roger de Piles in 1708 published a verbatim account of the use and misuse of sculpture after notes from Rubens' notebooks that he had in his possession:

"To reach the highest perfection it is necessary to understand [statues], indeed to drink them in; but they must be used with judgement and care taken that painting does not take on the quality of stone. For many inexperienced and even experienced artists do not distinguish the material from the form, the stone from the figure, or the requirements of the marble from those of art."

Rubens' use of statuary as inspiration, as well as the extent to which he was able to disguise his source and translate it into the fluid paint medium is well illustrated by the *Descent from the Cross* altarpiece (see page 35), painted for Antwerp Cathedral between 1611 and 1614, where the figures of Christ, St John and Nicodemus are directly inspired by the figures of the Hellenistic *Laocoön* group which he had copied in the Vatican gardens. Both the unmistakable formal similarity and the distance Rubens achieves from the original demonstrate graphically not only his dependence on other art to prompt his own inventions but also the measure of his artistic independence.

As early as 1611 Rubens was having to turn away prospective students and to refuse commissions, so overwhelmed was he by requests for work. He very soon established a large and highly organized workshop in his new residence. Otto Sperling, a Danish medical student, visited the house in 1621 and left a valuable record of his working methods. He found the painter "just at work, in the course of which he was read to from Tacitus and moreover dictating a letter. As we did not disturb him by talking, he began to speak to us, carrying on his work without stopping, still being read to and going on with his dictation." There is no reason to suggest that this conjuring-trick facility was assumed. Sperling also saw the assistants at work, "...all painting different pieces which had been sketched out by Mr Rubens with chalk and a

touch of paint here and there. The young fellows had to work up their pictures fully in oils until finally Mr Rubens himself would put the finishing touches with his own brushes. All this is considered Rubens' work; [and] thus he has gained a large fortune." Sperling clearly regarded Ruben's workshop as a kind of mass-production factory, and with some truth. Certainly Rubens had not time for the instruction of pupils in the strict sense. He employed apprentices to learn the trade step by step from the most menial tasks of grinding the colors and preparing the panels upwards. His most gifted assistants (including for a time the young Anthony van Dyck) were competent and sometimes very gifted painters in their own right, and Rubens was clearly dependent on them to a large degree in building up and thus interpreting, in a specifically "Rubenesque" manner, his initial designs. He would then alter or complete the top layers with a deft and personal hand, thus making them "autograph" (though he was always scrupulous in his business dealings in specifying the degree of studio help involved, and varied his prices accordingly).

In the years between 1610 and 1620 Rubens seems to have worked to the full, building up his reputation with a prodigious output which included altarpieces and whole cycles of paintings, as for example the decorations for the Jesuit Church in Antwerp, as well as smaller individually commissioned works, tapestry designs and even title pages of books.

The artist as diplomat

The next ten years might be characterized as Rubens' decade of diplomacy. In 1623 he was in Paris on behalf of the Regent Isabella; in 1626 he was again in France; in 1627 he visited Holland, and in 1628 Madrid, traveling thence in 1629 directly to England and returning home only in March 1630. During this time he succeeded in laying the basis for a peace treaty between England and Spain. Because of his singular position as painter first and diplomat second, his detachment from the courts and thus lack of political ambition, and his sincere desire for peace, he was trusted by all parties and acted as go-between in the delicate negotiations. He was knighted by both Charles I of England and Philip IV of Spain.

His wholehearted involvement in diplomatic activity and his continued absence from home was prompted by the death of his wife, probably of the plague, in 1626. His daughter, Clara Serena, had died three years earlier. Rubens wrote to a friend of his loss: "...since the true remedy for all ills is Forgetfulness, daughter of Time, I must without doubt look to her for help. But I find it very

RUBENS' PAINTING METHODS

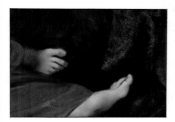

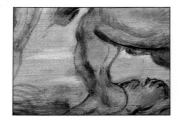

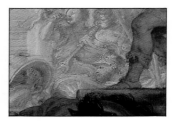

In this detail from Samson and Delilah *the transparent brown underpainting can be seen, left uncovered in places to form the middle ground.*

In the Lion Hunt, *one of Rubens' preliminary* modellos, *the white ground is visible beneath the yellow-brown under-painting.*

This detail of Rape of the Sabine Women *shows the contrast of brushwork, from thin washes to thick impasto.*

Although he sometimes used canvas, Rubens preferred to work on wooden panels, which gave a smooth surface and allowed his brush to move fluently. The panels, made by a professional panel maker, consisted of several oak planks glued together and then covered with a white ground made up of chalk bound with animal glue and impregnated with oil. This type of support was common at the time, but Rubens was distinctly innovative in his priming *(imprimatura)*, which consisted of very thin yellowish brown paint applied unevenly, usually in long, diagonal strokes from top right to bottom left. This underlayer, applied with a coarse bristle brush to create a striated effect and allow some of the white ground to show through, is clearly visible in Rubens' oil-sketches. It plays an important part in the color effects of the finished paintings, particularly in the flesh, where the transparent brown is sometimes left exposed to form the middle ground.

In general, Rubens did very little under-drawing on the support, since his practice was to execute a preliminary *modello* which provided the general layout for the painting. Instead, the composition was sketched in with thin, fluid paint, and the laying in of colors proceeded from this point, the lights being built up thickly to cover the ground priming and the shadows scumbled thinly over it. Rubens is described as painting with a pot of turpentine beside him, frequently dipping his brush into it to thin or work the paint (the first documented reference to turpentine as a diluent), which may help to explain the amazing variety of his brushwork.

This painting of Susanna Fourment, Rubens' first wife's sister, done about 1620, is one of his loveliest and most luminous portraits. His preference for wooden panels as a painting support allowed him considerably more latitude than canvas. The support for this painting consists of four oak planks made by a well-known panel maker, whose monogram is on the back. The composition appears to have expanded spontaneously from a central core, with two strips of wood added, one on the right to expand the sky and another at the bottom to give the figure more substance. Such a practice was not unusual for Rubens: in his Autumn Landscape with a View of Het Steen *(see page 55), painted on a support made up of seventeen panels, he appears to have enlarged the composition in several stages, adding strips to bottom, top and sides as he became more and more interested in the panoramic landscape.*

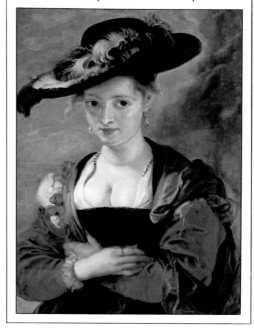

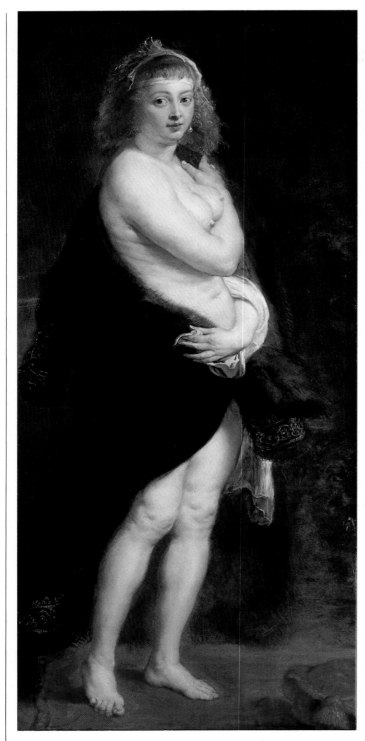

PETER PAUL RUBENS
Helena Fourment as Venus or
"Het Pelsken"
c 1636-8
Kunsthistorisches Museum,
Vienna

In this sumptuously painted
image of his second wife,
Rubens has posed her in the
attitude of the classical
"Medici Venus," and placed her

in front of a fountain, just
visible in the right
background. The idea of the
fur wrap was borrowed from
Titian. Neither simply a
portrait nor purely an image
of a mythological deity, this
intensely private work has
ironically become one of the
most celebrated erotic images
in Western art.

hard to separate grief from the memory of a person
whom I must love and cherish as long as I live."

The major works he painted during this period reflect
his political role as arbiter of kings and princely propagandist. In 1622 he was summoned to France by Marie
de' Medici, the widow of King Henry IV. After her husband's assassination in 1610 she had been appointed
regent to her son, Louis XIII, until he ousted his mother
from power and assumed the full position of king in
1620. Two years later Marie de' Medici commissioned
Rubens to decorate two long galleries in the Luxembourg Palace with a series of twenty-one huge canvases,
celebrating her life and virtues, a subject that clearly
presented something of a challenge even to Rubens.

In the largest surviving cycle of monumental canvases (see page 43) he skillfully conjoined pagan and
Christian imagery, actual incident and allegory, to rein-
force the somewhat sparse glories of her reign. The work
took three years to complete, and assistants were used
extensively in realizing the vast designs.

During this period his style loosened considerably,
the hard outlines and sculptural modeling of form
diminished and his treatment became more painterly,
with the colors warmer and more saturated and the
compositions more complex. All these tendencies are to
be seen in the sumptuous *Allegory of Peace and War* (see
page 50), which Rubens presented to Charles I before
leaving England and which neatly summed up the purpose of his mission.

The later years

On his return to Antwerp in March 1630 he made a clear
decision to leave political life. Partly exasperated by the
fickle and vacillating habits of negotiators and their
masters, partly discomfited by personal slights and
financial losses meted out to him by the Spanish
bureaucracy, and partly spurred on by the promptings of
the creative instincts that had had of necessity to lie
fairly dormant, he persuaded the Regent Isabella to
release him from further diplomatic assignments. In
December of that year, at the age of fifty-three, he married again, taking as his wife Helena Fourment, the six-
teen-year-old daughter of an Antwerp silk merchant. He
frankly explained his reason for doing so to an old friend:
"...since I was not yet inclined to live the life of a celibate
thinking that, if we must give the first place to contin-
ence we may enjoy licit pleasures with thankfulness...I
have taken a young wife of honest but middle-class
family..." The many paintings of Helena in a variety of
guises — as Venus or as Hagar in the Wilderness — as well

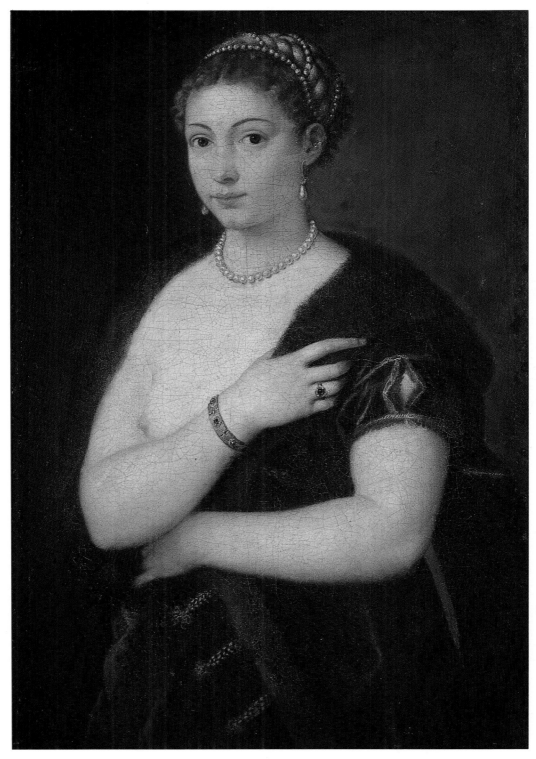

TITIAN
Girl in a Fur Wrap
1535-7
Kunsthistorisches Museum,
Vienna

Rubens made a copy of this
painting when he saw it in the
collection of Charles I, and
later used the erotic idea of a
partially draped wrap for his
own "*Het Pelsken*." The subject
of the Titian painting was an
anonymous girl, intended as a
mildly erotic "pin-up" of a
type readily available in his
workshop. The same model
reappears in a similar pose
and wearing the same blue
dress in a painting bought by
Francesco Maria della Rovere
in 1536, now in the Pitti
Palace, Florence.

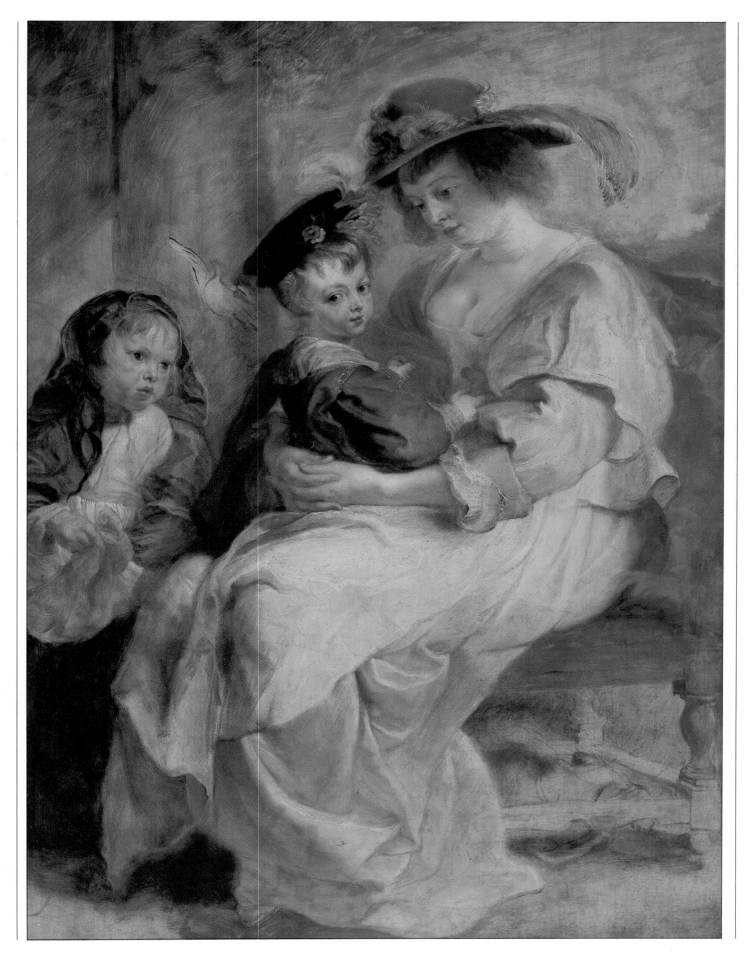

as straight portraits, clearly reveal the extent to which she was his inspiration and the object of an almost palpable physical passion.

Equally inspirational for his late paintings was the example of Titian, never far below the surface throughout his career, but a powerful instrument in the deepening of his own style in the last decade of his life. Like the late works of Titian or Rembrandt, his style becomes deeply personal, and though aided considerably by a renewed study of Titian, the loosening of style is the product of a lifetime's handling and experience with paint. The beautiful and sumptuous *Het Pelsken*, or *Helena Fourment as Venus*, shows the twin aspects of his passion: the physical beauty of his wife expressed in the warm diaphanous brushwork inspired by the Venetian master, which allows him to create the opalescent glow of soft skin. The subject has its basis in Titian's *Girl in a Fur Wrap*, but Rubens has made the idea completely his own. Unlike Titian, who generalizes his forms, Rubens sees no need to disguise the dimples and puckers of the knees or the folds of flesh under the arm. He combines the dignity of a goddess with a human and fleshly eroticism. This work had a special significance for the artist and his wife, for he expressly left it to her in his will, calling it "Het Pelsken" or "The Little Fur," and though she destroyed several nudes after his death, she spared this one.

In 1635 he bought the large castle of Steen, near Malines, and to all intents and purposes retired there. Though he was kept busy throughout the 1630s with "official" commissions, notably the finishing of the Whitehall ceiling canvases (1634), the city decorations for the triumphal entry into Antwerp of the Cardinal Infante Ferdinand (1635), and unceasing demands from the Spanish king, in general his subject matter becomes more personal, the style more relaxed, and he seems to be painting more for pleasure. The warm and vibrant landscapes of the countryside around his estate (see page 59) suggest an enjoyment in depicting the things closest to him, as do the group portraits of his family. Though increasingly hampered by gout, he lost none of his powers of invention or precision of touch. The *Rape of the Sabine Women* (see page 55) of c 1635 illustrates his skill in organizing large numbers of figures into an expressive and intelligible whole and by a brilliance of touch and color, to endow the energy of his compositions with profound poetic vision.

His last great self-portrait (see page 6) must date from the last five years of his life. It combines the outwardly worldly — the pose, costume and background pillar show the traditional attributes of the distinguished statesman — with acute self-knowledge: the honesty with which he describes the tired and slackening features underlines the pervasive sense of gravitas and sharp intelligence. It constitutes a profound summation and testament of his life.

Rubens died in Antwerp on May 30, 1640. Though the use of allegory and frequent references to obscure classical myths or episodes from forgotten Roman history make his works today often difficult to digest, no other artist before or since has equaled his ability to employ brushstrokes both to describe form and to endow it with such a buoyancy and vibrant sense of energy. Above all, his idea of truth, his affirmation of human feelings and emotion is expressed in terms of movement, be it in the overall dynamic vehemence of his compositional formuli or in the rapid sequences of broken brushwork. Unlike his younger contemporary Rembrandt, who sought to express in his figures an idea of inner truth almost at the expense of the material world, Rubens, one might say, believed that truth lay not at the bottom of a well, but on the surface, traceable in the outward appearance of things. It is in the joyful apprehending of this sensual world that his peculiar greatness lies.

PETER PAUL RUBENS
Helena Fourment and her Children
c 1636
Louvre, Paris

This family group of Rubens' wife and children demonstrates the breadth and informality of his late work. It is unfinished, as can be seen from the lower part of the stool, which remains unpainted. The two hands that protrude into the right side of the picture belong to the third child, Isabella, as is known from a preparatory drawing in the Louvre, and reveal that the painting has been cut down at some later date.

CHRONOLOGY OF RUBENS' LIFE

1577   June 28: born at Siegen, Westphalia to Jan and Maria.

1578   Moves with family to Cologne.

1587   Father dies; family moves to Antwerp.

1590   Becomes page to the Countess de Ligne.

1591-2   Works in studio of Tobias Verhaecht, then apprenticed to Adam van Noort.

c 1596   Moves to studio of Otto van Veen (Vaenius).

1598   Master in Antwerp Guild of St Luke.

1600-3   Paints *Judgement of Paris*. Leaves Antwerp for Italy, then Spain. Attends proxy marriage of Marie de' Medici to Henri IV in Florence (1600).

1604   Returns to Mantua via Genoa.

1605   Completes paintings for SS. Trinita, Mantua.

1606-7   In Genoa and Rome. Completes first Chiesa Nova altarpiece.

1608   Leaves Rome on news of mother's illness, but mother dead on return.

1609   Paints *Samson and Delilah*, and *Adoration of the Kings* for Antwerp town hall. September: appointed court painter to the Regents. October: marries Isabella Brant. Twelve Years' Truce begins.

1610-12   Begins building new house and workshop. Commission for St Walburga altarpiece and *Deposition* altarpiece.

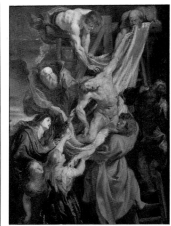

The Descent from the Cross

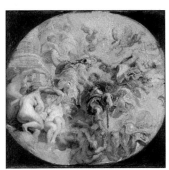

The Duke of Buckingham Conducted to the Temple of Virtus

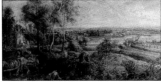

Autumn Landscape with a View of Het Steen

1620-1   Paints ceilings for Antwerp Jesuit church. Twelve Years' Truce ends.

1622   In Paris. Commission for *Marie de' Medici* cycle.

1623   In Paris again with nine completed *Marie de' Medici* pictures.

1624   *Adoration of Kings* for St Michael, Antwerp.

1625   Meets Duke of Buckingham and sells paintings to him.

1626   Isabella Brant dies.

1628   Paints *Madonna and Saints* for St Augustine, Antwerp. Leaves for Madrid.

1629   Brussels via Paris, then London. Paints *Allegory of Peace and War* for Charles I. Knighted by Charles I at Whitehall.

1630   Leaves political life. Marries Helena Fourment.

1634   Continues work on Whitehall ceilings. Paints *Rape of the Sabine Women*.

1635   Buys castle of Steen near Malines. Suffers increasingly from gout. Completes Whitehall ceilings and city decorations for entry into Antwerp of Cardinal-Infante Ferdinand. Paints landscapes.

1636   Appointed court painter to Cardinal-Infante Ferdinand.

c 1639   Paints last *Self-portrait*.

1640   May 30: dies in Antwerp, buried in St James'.

THE PAINTINGS

THE JUDGEMENT OF PARIS

c 1600
52¾×68¾in/134×174.5cm
Oil on panel
National Gallery, London

This painting is one of Rubens' earliest surviving works, executed in about 1600, in all probability shortly before he left for Italy. It represents, in figure style and palette, the culmination of his apprenticeship in the idiom of late Flemish Mannerism.

The scene depicts the pastoral beauty contest between Juno, Minerva and Venus, judged by Paris, the son of King Priam of Troy, who had been abandoned to die on a hillside as a baby following a prophecy that he would bring about the ruin of Troy. Raised by a shepherd, he eventually married Oenone, the daughter of the river god Oneus, both of whom are to be seen on the right-hand side of the painting. Angered that she was not invited to the wedding, Eris the goddess of Strife threw down a golden apple among the guests, inscribed "To the fairest." Paris, decreed by Jupiter to be the judge, was offered lands and wealth by Juno, and victory in battle by Minerva, while Venus offered him the love of the most beautiful mortal woman, Helen of Sparta.

Though Rubens' initial idea, as preparatory drawings and an oil-sketch make clear, had been to show Paris in the process of choosing, instructing the goddesses to disrobe, he changed this first and more purely erotic conception to the dramatic and "historically" more crucial moment when Paris awarded the golden apple to Venus, thereby initiating the process that was to lead to his abduction of Helen and the Trojan War. The epic nature of this act is made clear by the *putti* who place a wreath upon Venus' head, amid a burst of celestial light.

Rubens used Marcantonio Raimondi's print (opposite) of Raphael's own *Judgement of Paris* as a starting point for the central figure group, although the figure of Venus has been much altered. It is possible too that Paris' muscular back implies some knowledge of the Hellenistic sculpture known as the "Belvedere Torso," perhaps through prints or plaster casts. These references show the artist attempting to come to terms with Italian and antique art, even at secondhand.

The artificiality of the stylized poses is increased by the vivid and discordant contrasts of color between the gleaming, marble-like flesh tones and the green-blue background, heightened by the harsh red and mauve accents at the extremities of flesh. The treatment of the river god and his daughter show clearly Rubens' method of building up the flesh tones. The thin striated umber underpainting is visible in the god's chest, running diagonally from top left to bottom right. The outlines and general musculature have been sketched in on top in a darker brown — probably raw umber. The flesh tints of pink, blue and an orange-yellow were then painted on top in fluid sequence. The outlines of the hands have been drawn in in bright red. These figures are the most thinly painted areas of the whole work, and allow the painting process to be clearly seen. The treatment of flesh is essentially the same in the main figures, although to a more developed degree. The colors used are startling in their range: from a turquoise-greenish blue to a dark red lake to lemon yellow. Hot reds are used in thicker accents for the nipples, navel outlines and shadows under the arms and around the buttocks.

The painting of the cloud and *putti* above Venus' head is very thickly applied and probably disguises earlier ideas painted out at a later stage. The disturbing contrast between the lemon yellow and purple is characteristically Flemish. To appreciate Rubens' adoption of a more Italianate palette and the maturing of his figure style, it is instructive to compare this early work with, for example, the *Allegory of Peace and War* (see page 50), painted some twenty-nine years later, both for the overall tonality and the treatment of flesh.

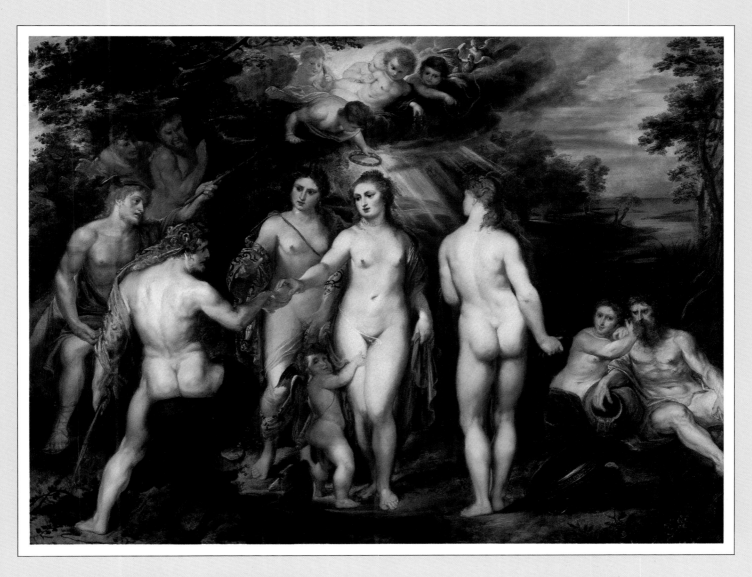

This is one of Rubens' earliest surviving works, and clearly shows the influence of Mannerist Flemish painting in the smooth, enamel-like modeling and the palette of acid and discordant colors. The figural composition is derived from Italian prints, especially the one shown here, an engraving after Raphael's treatment of the same subject. This formed the starting point for the painting, although the figure of Venus has been much altered.

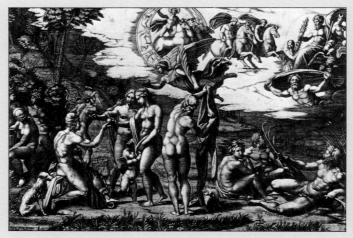

MARCANTONIO RAIMONDI
The Judgement of Paris
(after Raphael)
British Museum, London

Raimondi was one of the first Italian artists to make a living solely as an engraver. His career began in Venice, where he copied Dürer's prints, but he later moved to Rome and devoted himself to reproducing designs by Raphael. His engravings formed one of the main channels through which Italian ideas were transmitted to other parts of Europe.

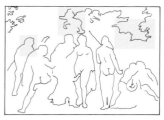

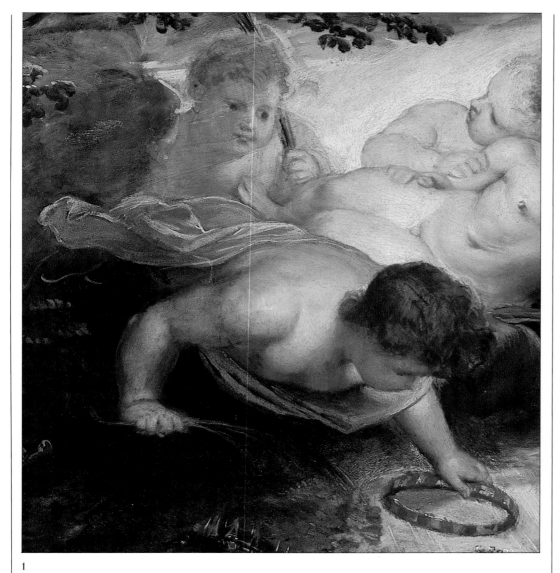

1

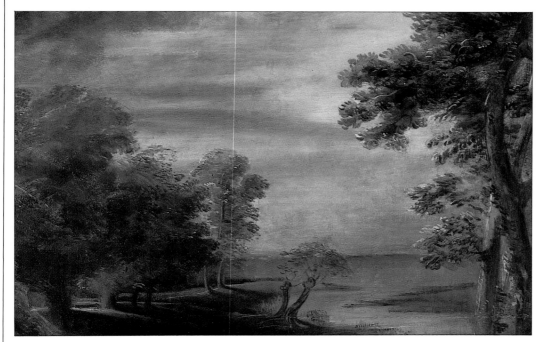

2

1 The flesh tones of the *putti* show the young Rubens' predilection for a rather loud palette. Here he has used a pale flesh tone in combination with a harsh turquoise green, a bright vermilion (in the nipples and outlines) and touches of yellow. The passage of bright lemon yellow behind the group sets off the colors in almost garish contrast. This area is very thickly painted, covering an earlier idea.

2 This combination of aqueous turquoise greens and blues is typical of the palette of the Flemish landscape painters of the later sixteenth century. Here the colors have been very thinly applied in broad washes, with details of the trees and river bank lightly sketched over this in brown or black paint. The foliage of the right-hand tree has been freely worked in loose dabs of varying tones of green and brown. The crack running horizontally through this section shows where the planks that make up the panel have parted slightly.

3 *Actual size detail* The head of Mercury clearly shows Rubens' early flesh-painting technique. It is very thinly painted in rather subdued tones, thus allowing the more brightly lit figure of Paris to assume greater prominence. The thin bluish gray colors have been applied over the umber underpainting and are set off by touches of bright crimson in the cheeks, lips and nostril.

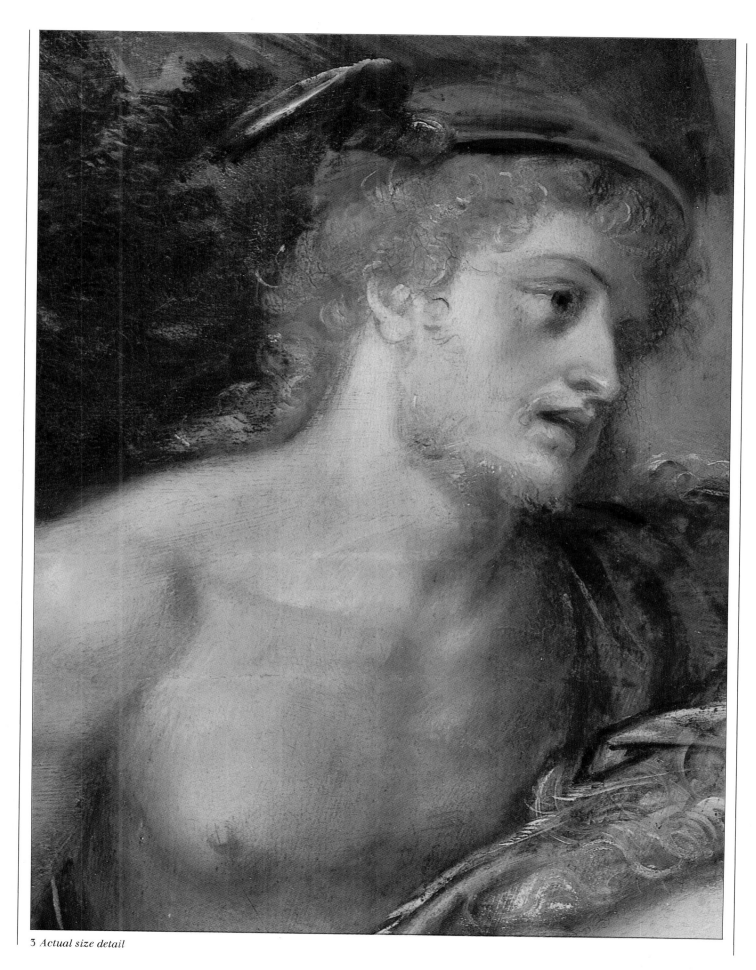

3 *Actual size detail*

THE ARTIST AND HIS WIFE
IN A HONEYSUCKLE BOWER

c 1609-10
$68\frac{1}{2} \times 52$in/174×132cm
Oil on canvas
Alte Pinakothek, Munich

Shortly after his return from Italy in 1609, Rubens married Isabella Brant, the eighteen-year old daughter of Jan Brant who, together with Rubens' elder brother Philip, was one of the four Secretaries of the City. Philip had married the sister-in-law of Jan Brant some six months earlier. In a sense marriage symbolized for Rubens a kind of coming-of-age, a decision to settle down after a nine-year absence from his home town.

This double portrait was probably painted shortly after the wedding to commemorate the event, and the theme of shared love runs appropriately throughout, most obviously in the pose of the seated couple, who sit holding hands. This follows a fairly common theme in earlier northern marriage portraits. The very deliberate nature of the gesture contains something of the seriousness of an exchange of vows, and it is interesting to note that the same motif of clasped hands was used as a symbol of faithful love in emblem books of the seventeenth century. Furthermore, the couple are seated beneath a flowering honeysuckle bush, symbolic of fruitful love.

The work is thinly painted with a smooth, descriptive brush, the volumes of the forms firmly modeled, and the planes of the faces articulated by delicate transitions of tone. Great attention is given to details of lace and clothing and to the rendering of different textures and materials — all executed with a minuteness of touch that relates back to Rubens' Flemish training.

The colors employed are cool and rather sober, with a predominance of flat, rather muddy hues. The dark tonality of the painting is the result of a warm brown underpainting, visible in the foreground and modifying the blue of the sky on the left-hand side. It occurs also as the middle tone of Rubens' jacket front. In general the paint is applied very thinly. The texture of the canvas can be seen in the straw hat, where it helps convey the rough texture of the material, and is also visible in the shadowed area of Isabella's brow. The flesh tones of her face have been marvelously built up by subtle glazes of pinks and modified whites, and darker brown for the heavier shadows, applied over a general flesh color.

No details are known of Isabella's life. The only reference to her is in a letter written by Rubens after her death in 1626, in which he describes her as "an excellent companion, whom one could love, indeed had to love with good reason — as having none of the faults of her sex. She had no capricious moods, and no feminine weaknesses, but was all goodness and honesty. And because of her virtues she was loved during her lifetime, and mourned by all at her death." In this portrait Rubens has drawn her as it were from the "outside." Her neat, modest features are delicately and accurately described, but as yet without knowledge of the inner person, unlike the ravishing portrait drawing of her done some twenty-two years later (opposite), where Rubens has portrayed a full personality, capturing her tender, complicit smile as husband draws her. Fuller knowledge of the sitter, as well as a facility with his materials borne of years of experience separates the two portrayals, showing up the youthful nature of this early work without in any way diminishing its obvious virtuosity and genius.

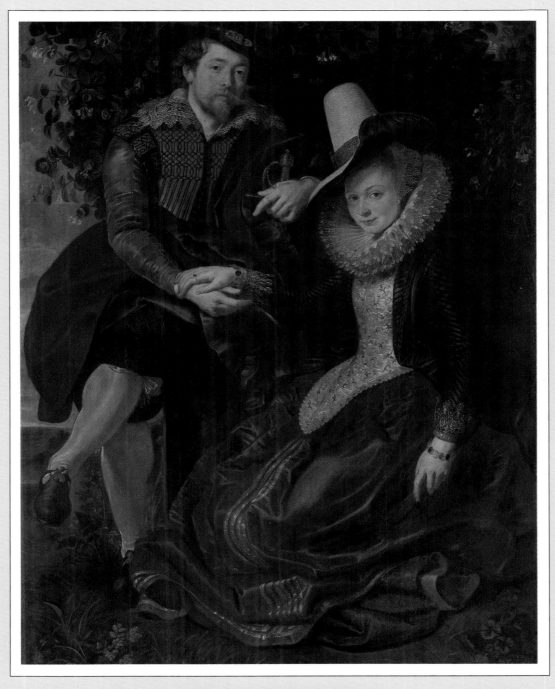

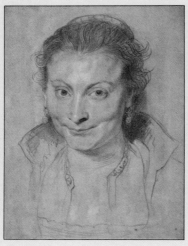

This painting was probably done soon after Rubens' marriage to Isabella Brant to commemorate the event. It is an excellent example of Rubens' concern for the careful depiction of different textures, particularly noticeable in the masterly painting of the ruff and in the straw hat, the texture of which has been produced by manipulating the rough grain of the canvas and gently criss-crossing it with white and yellow-tinted cross-hatchings.

Isabella Brant
c 1622
British Museum, London

This ravishing drawing is a wonderful example of Rubens' mature drawing style, and makes an interesting comparison with the double portrait, painted at the beginning of the marriage. He evokes the warm personality of the sitter by the most economical of means, and breathes life into the smile and movement into the expression.

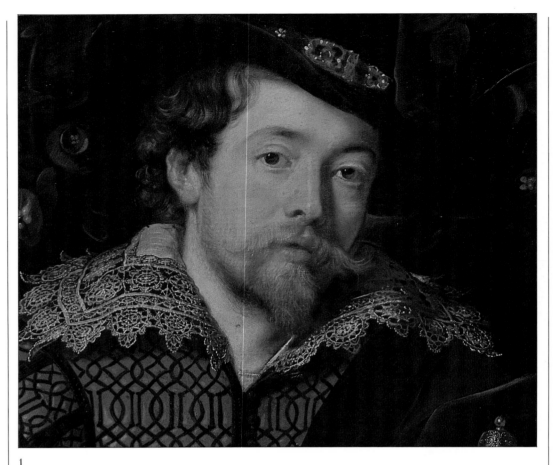

1

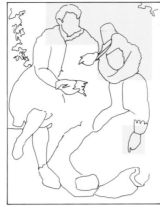

1 The flesh tones here are thinly applied, with the brown underpaint quite clearly visible in parts of the face, particularly around the extremities and in the areas of light shadow. The right cheek shows Rubens' ability to create subtle gradations of tone by building up thin layers of different flesh colors, from pink to orange and beige, over the underlying strokes of umber that define the cheekbone.

2 The subtle transitions of tone have been achieved by building up delicate layers of flesh tones of slightly different values, brushed fairly broadly over the burnt umber outline and shadowing that emerge at chin, jaw and eyebrow and solidly define the planes of the face. The lace ruff is a delicate piece of descriptive painting, the fall of light beautifully placed by the minute touches of white impasto.

3 *Actual size detail* Compared to the treatment of the other hands in the painting, this is broadly painted, with the underpaint clearly visible in the deeper shadows, and an orange-brown both defining the outlines and providing a middle tone. Tinted white highlights have been roughly scumbled on top to describe the brightest reflections.

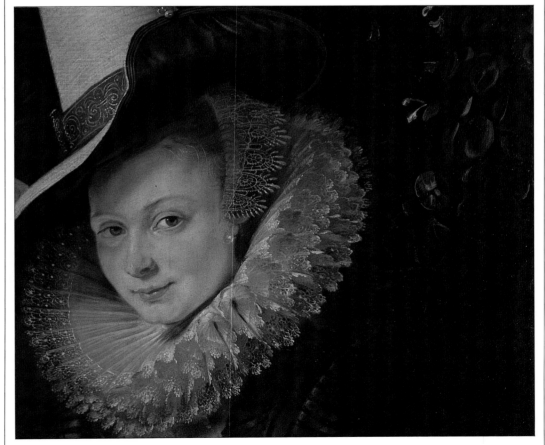

2

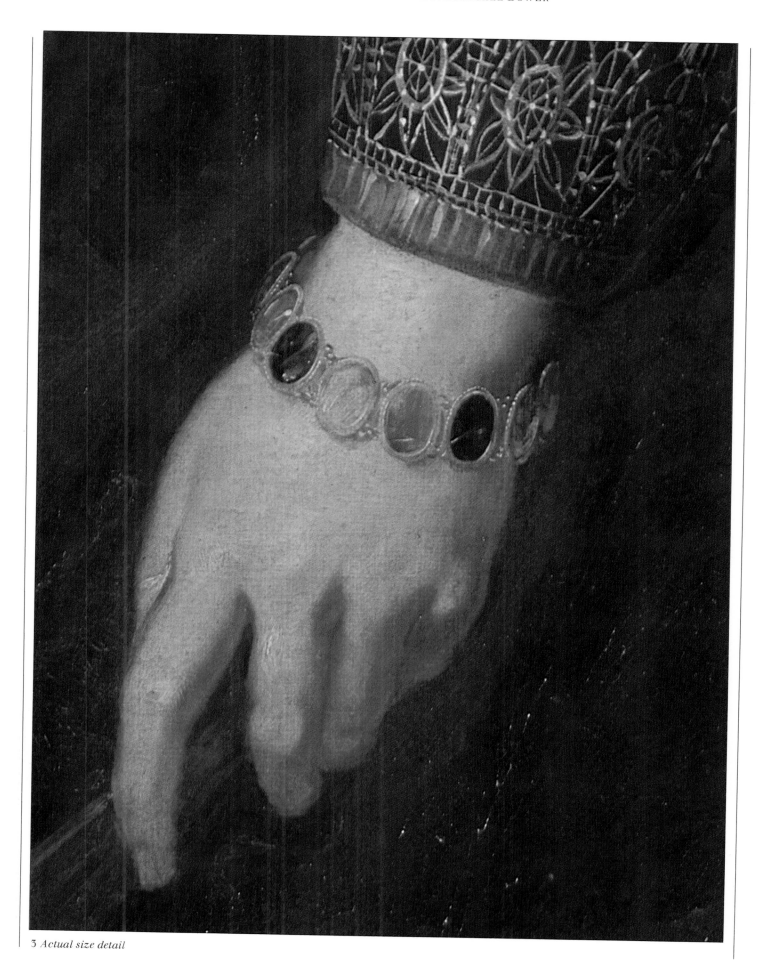

3 *Actual size detail*

SAMSON AND DELILAH

c1609
72¾×80¾in/185×205cm
Oil on panel
National Gallery, London

Rubens was commissioned to paint this large panel-painting in about 1609, shortly after his return from Italy. His patron was Nicholas Rickox, a prominent Antwerp citizen and personal friend of the painter, who as president of the Guild of Arquebusiers was probably responsible for Ruben's commission from that guild to paint the *Descent from the Cross* in Antwerp cathedral (see page 35). From an extant painting by Frans Francken the Younger, it is known that the *Samson and Delilah* hung in a prominent position above the large mantelpiece in Rickox' salon, and from the general perspective within the painting, which necessitates a fairly low viewing point, it is clear that Rubens painted it with this location in mind.

The coloring is extremely rich although the range of colors is limited and a restricted palette has been used. The main areas of paint are thinly applied and have survived in almost pristine condition, with very little paint loss — a testimony to Rubens' craftsmanship and his use of old-established methods. The support is an oak panel, made up of six horizontal planks glued together, and supplied in all likelihood by a professional panel-maker. Following fifteenth-century Flemish precedent, Rubens generally preferred wooden supports, for unlike canvas, the smooth surface allowed his brush to move more fluently. This was then covered with a white ground made up of chalk bound in animal glue. Over it Rubens painted a thin *imprimatura* in light yellow-brown paint, which runs for the most part diagonally from top right to bottom left. It was applied very thinly, using a coarse hog-hair brush to create a striated effect, which allowed the white ground to show through. It is an effect particularly characteristic of his oil-sketches. This transparent brown is left exposed in the finished painting to form the middle ground in such areas as — most spectacularly — Delilah's right wrist and upper hand, Samson's

right calf and upper leg, and passages of Delilah's yellow drapery.

There would have been very little underdrawing, as the preliminary *modello* provided the general layout. One or two bold strokes of black, visible for instance along Samson's wrist, his shadowed underarm and the folds of Delilah's white sleeve, were used to establish the general disposition of the figures. The laying-in of colors would have proceeded progressively from this point. The dark background is very sketchily painted, in striking contrast to the main foreground group, the architectural details mapped out in rough strokes of translucent reddish-brown, and painted directly over the thin priming, as are the local colors of the soldiers. Both the reflected highlights on the soldiers' armor and legs and the candle flame are applied in thicker impastoed strokes on top.

The same warm reddish-brown occurs in other areas of shadow, notably in Samson's back, and suggests that Rubens began with the background area and mapped out the areas of shadow with the same color in the foreground at the same time. The flesh tones were then thinly applied on top, modifying the shadowed areas. The basic pink flesh tones of Delilah's skin are made up of lead white tinted with vermilion, with the highlights a mixture of lead white and a little yellow ocher. Deeper effects of shadow, as between Delilah's breasts and along Samson's upper arm, are laid in with warm red-brown glazes similar to those of the background.

The passages of drapery are dazzlingly broad and direct in treatment. The red dress is made up of broad strokes of crimson lake mixed with tinges of vermilion, the deeper shadows created with glazes of crimson lake superimposed on top. The highlights are in strokes of lead white, softened also by crimson-lake glazes. Tinges of orange yellow to suggest reflections of the candle flame are visible in the folds of Delilah's lap.

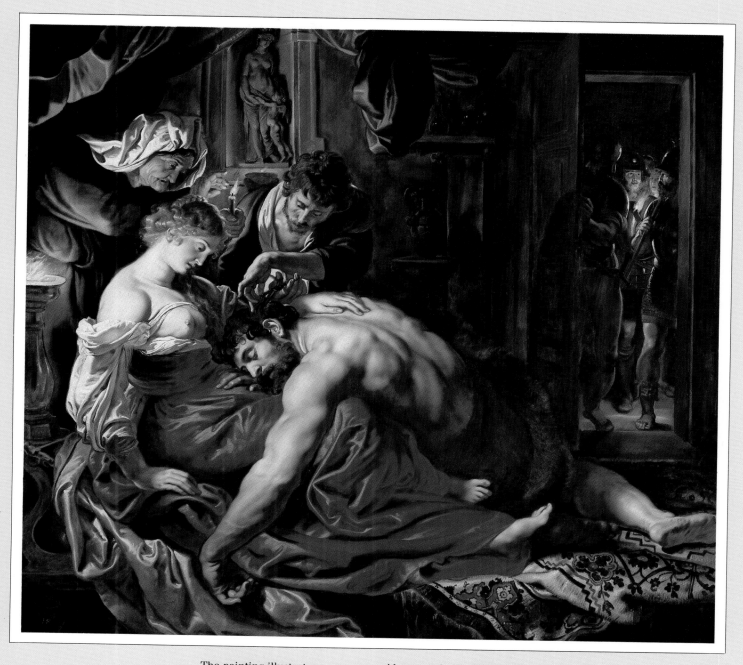

The painting illustrates Samson's betrayal by Delilah who, having elicited from him the knowledge that his superhuman strength lies in his hair, seduces him and has his hair shorn while he sleeps. The erotic treatment, emphasizing woman's power over man, is typical of the seventeenth century, and the statuette of a blindfolded Venus further comments on the theme of "blind love." The old woman holding the taper represents a procuress, thus locating the scene in a brothel. The forms of the central group reflect Rubens' study of Italian art. The figure of Delilah is derived from the pose of Leda in Michelangelo's lost work, *Leda and the Swan*, while Samson's massive, muscular back also contains echoes of Michelangelo and of the antique.

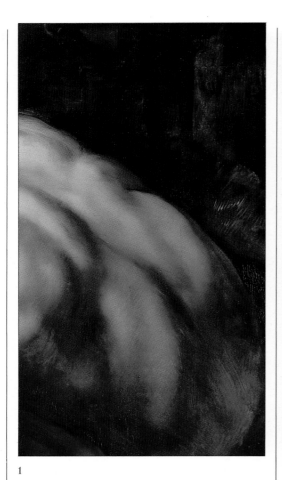

1

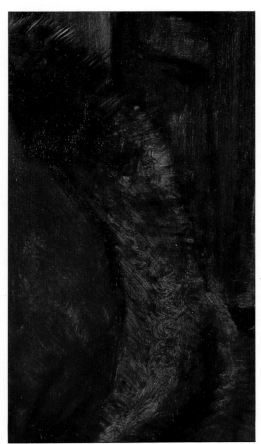

2

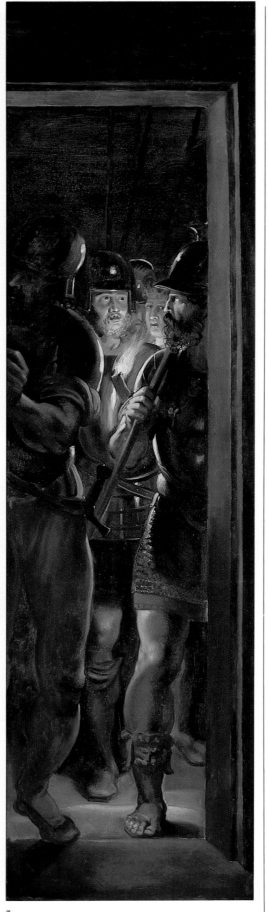

3

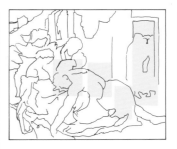

1 This detail illustrates Rubens' method of working up his form from a warm medium brown. The main planes of the back have been drawn in burnt umber, with the deep shadows applied around them in brown wash. Increasingly lighter flesh tones have then been built up, with the harsh transitions of tone modified with a neutral gray-green.

2 The outlines of the fur were first drawn in irregular streaks of burnt umber, after which the illusion of texture was created by dragging the same fluid paint in short, curling strokes, perhaps with a rag or broad brush. Strokes of dull, muddy green were laid on top, with individual hairs evoked by tiny strokes of yellow.

3 The whole area of the doorway and adjacent wall was initially painted in a warm brown, with the figures and the space they occupy suggested by bold streaks of color laid over it. The palette is muted and the tonality dark, in order to preserve the balance with the central figures.

4 The main planes of Samson's face were drawn in burnt umber, with a mid-tone applied over it and the brightest points confidently brushed in on top. The servant's jerkin appears to be blue, but is in fact made up of red lake, lead white and black, with no blue pigment used.

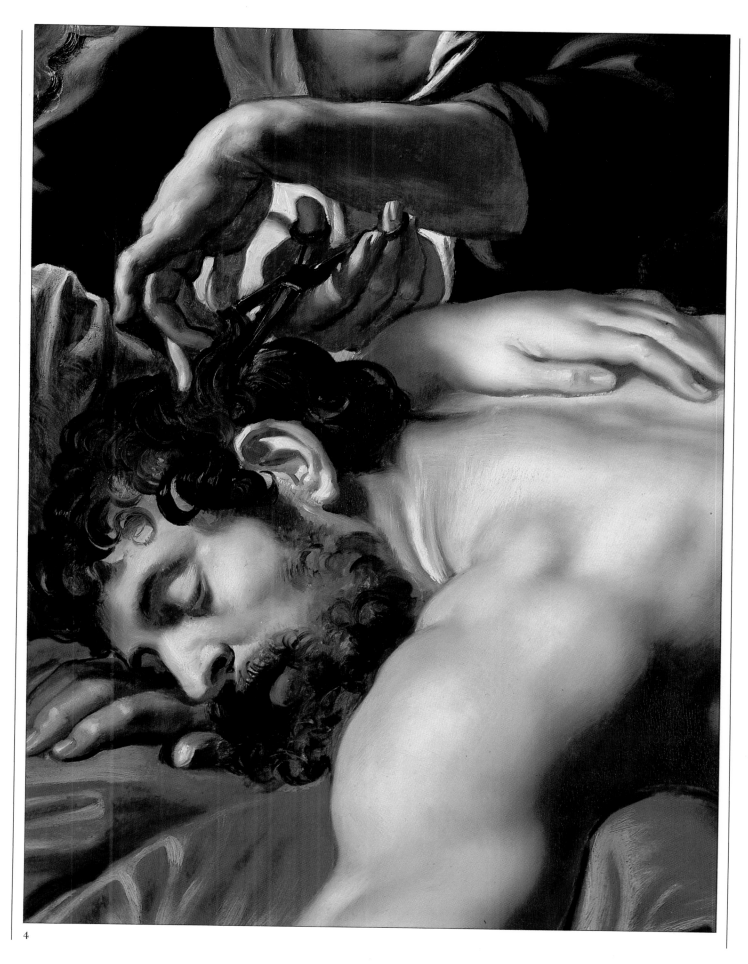

THE DESCENT FROM THE CROSS

1611-14

45×30in/114.3×76.2cm

Oil on panel

Courtauld Institute Galleries, London

This is a highly finished *modello* for one of the first major commissions Rubens received on his return to Antwerp. It was ordered by the Guild of Arquebusiers in 1611 for an altarpiece in their chapel in Antwerp Cathedral. This is the design for the central panel of the altar, which in its finished form is flanked by two wings which show the *Visitation* and the *Presentation in the Temple*. All the scenes chosen bear on the theme of Christ "being borne" in some way, and this iconographical connection is made clear on the exterior panels which show St Christopher, the guild's patron saint, whose name means literally "Christ-bearing." The high finish of the *modello* suggests that it was intended to be shown to the patrons for approval before work on the actual altarpiece panel began.

The commission arose from pressure placed upon the guild by the Church authorities to redecorate their chapel as part of a general move to renovate the whole building. It reflects the increasing spiritual regeneration of the Catholic Church in this period, though the six years Rubens had to wait for payment after delivery of the finished work suggest a less zealous attitude on the part of the financially hard-pressed guild. At any rate the altarpiece must fully have satisfied the Church authorities' desire for a new kind of art that would rekindle the worshiper's emotions and stir him to empathy and awe.

All the elements of the painting are directed toward the expression of a single, intense emotion. The figures are locked into a closed, self-contained group, joined together physically and psychologically by a complex interlacing of differing gestures, postures and expressions that centers on the dead body of Christ, but which is dominated by a single dramatic, sweeping movement that begins with the top right-hand bearer and continues diagonally down through the sheet, the figure of Christ, and ends in the group of grieving women at his feet. This generalized movement echoes the central forms of the dead Christ and thus extends the mood of heroic pathos throughout the composition. It shows Rubens' ability to use abstract pictorial devices — in this case a kind of contained movement — as a metaphor for a similar vehement motion of the spirit.

The figures of Christ, St John and Nicodemus are derived from the antique *Laocoön* group (see page 11). The modeling of the figures is also boldly sculptural, articulated by the strong directional lighting that enters from the top right-hand side of the panel. Moreover, the grouping of the figures into a self-contained block owes more to the principles of sixteenth-century sculpture than to those of traditional narrative painting, where the various figures, particularly the mourners at the foot of the cross, are normally separated into discrete groups.

The *modello* is very freely painted. The brown priming is visible in various parts of the painting: it forms the middle tones of the torso and of the face of Christ. The shadows that describe the muscles have been drawn in in a darker umber tone and then modified by a light flesh tone, probably made up of lead white mixed with yellow ocher, which produces the death-like pallor. The sheet also reveals traces of brown underpaint beneath the thin sequence of light, gray-white strokes. Broad thick strokes of white impasto laid on top indicate the folds which catch and reflect the light. Smudges of crimson vividly convey the blood that stains the sheet and runs down Christ's side and arms. The suggestive freedom of these marks is in striking contrast to exquisite details such as the tiny drop of white impasto that suggests the Virgin's tear-filled eyes. The draperies are painted with much the same freedom as those in the *Samson and Delilah* (see page 31), and the free and loose application of the brushstrokes contributes greatly to the overall sense of movement.

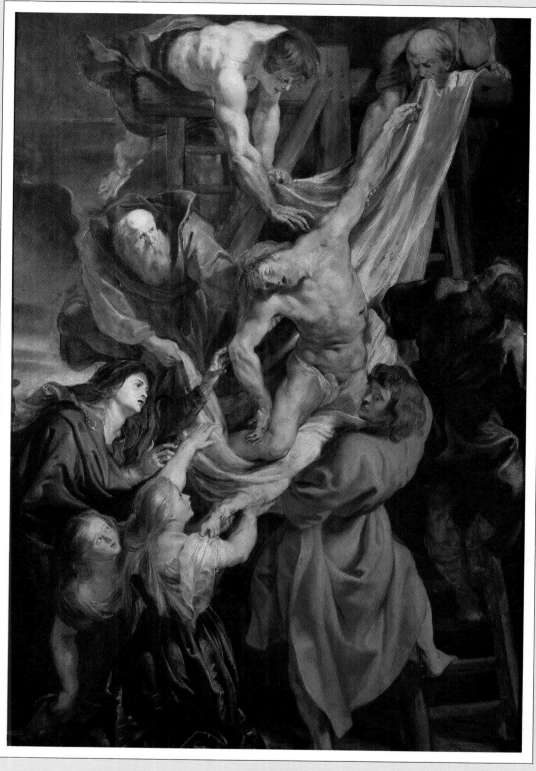

Rubens was a devout Catholic, who could paint religious scenes for churches with as much conviction as he painted works glorifying kings and noblemen. This work is a highly finished *modello* for his first major commission after his return to Antwerp, an altarpiece for the Guild of Arquebusiers' chapel in Antwerp Cathedral. The *Descent* forms the centerpiece of the altar, with the flanking wings showing the *Visitation* and the *Presentation in the Temple*. Although the *modello* is more akin to a finished painting than some of Rubens' others, such as the *Lion Hunt* (see page 39), it is very freely painted, for example the brown priming is visible in various parts of the work, forming the mid-tones, and the draperies have been treated with loose, suggestive brushstrokes. The idealized sense of form and the grand rhetoric of the poses are typical of Rubens' style at this period, and show the influence of sculpture on his work.

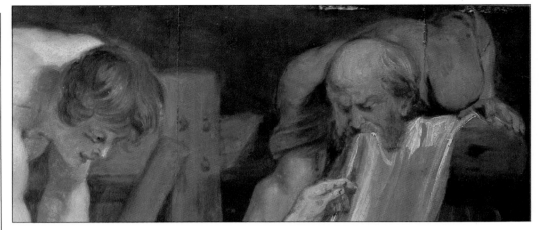

1

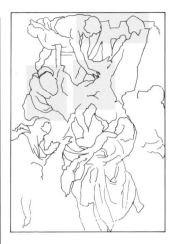

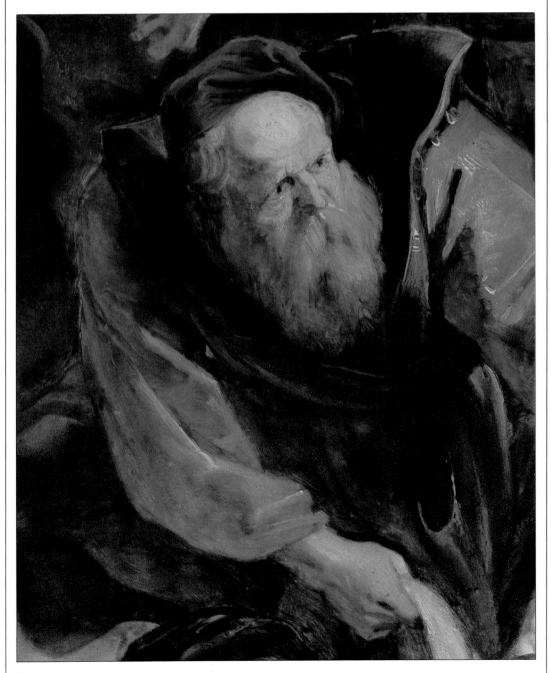

2

1 Rubens' method of building up his figures can be well seen in these two heads. Beginning with a transparent brown glaze over a white gesso ground, he has drawn the outlines in umber and brushed in the areas of shadow with a wash of the same color. Flesh tones of increasing lightness have then been applied in vigorous brushstrokes that follow the form of the muscles they describe.

2 The face of the old man illustrates how Rubens could enunciate exact details of form, expression and texture from the simplest elements. The right side of the face is hardly more than suggested by fluid strokes of brown wash, but the texture of aging skin is evoked by the uneven troughs the brushstrokes have left in the thin paint. The hairs of the beard, too, emerge from the rough underpaint by only the loosest of suggestions of individual hairs.

3 *Actual size detail* The moving image of the dead Christ's face is achieved with startling simplicity through stark contrasts of tone. These are created by a brown wash on the shadowed part and a light gray-ocher flesh tone for the areas in the light, heightened by touches of pure white on cheek, nostril, mouth and brow. The very roughness of the paint application contributes to the sense of pathos.

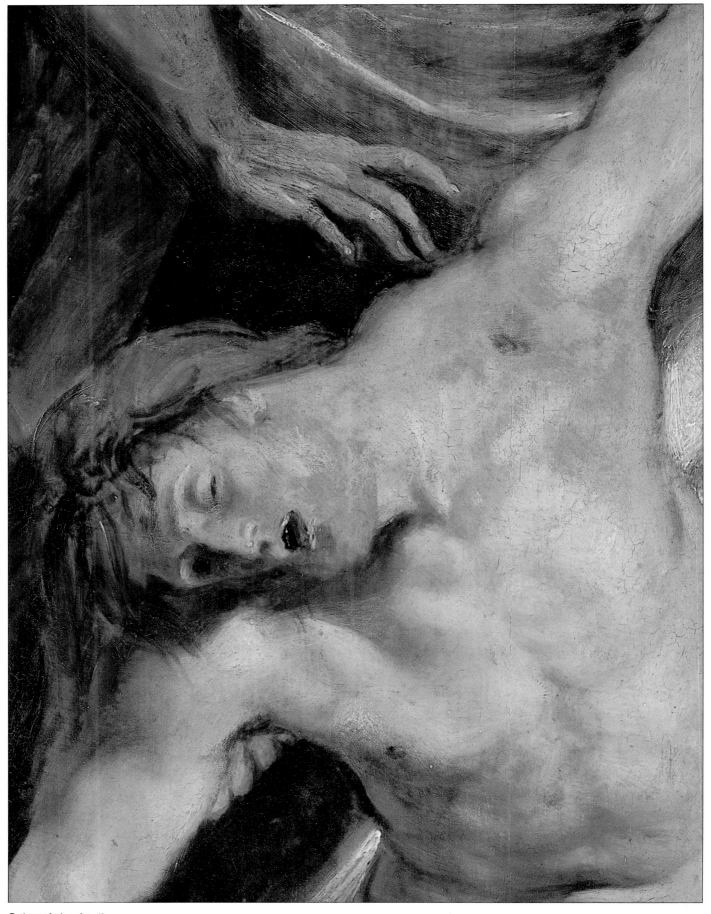

3 *Actual size detail*

Lion Hunt

c 1615
29×41½in/74×105.5cm
Oil on panel
National Gallery, London

This sketch was probably the starting point for a composition of a *Lion and Tiger Hunt* executed for Maximilian, Duke of Bavaria, and delivered in 1617. Rubens painted several large-scale hunting scenes during these years, which included, among other animals, hippopotamuses, crocodiles and wild boars. Such works were avidly sought after by a hunting nobility, who regarded them as exotic decorations for their country houses and palaces.

This small *modello* is important on a number of counts. In the first place it represents an important stage in Rubens' working process, showing how even at the earliest stages of conception he preferred to use an oil-sketch on a wooden panel to work out his ideas rather than following normal precedents and sketching on paper. The lack of colors makes it clear that this is just such an exploratory sketch and not a finished *modello* to be used by assistants, as does, even more obviously, the outline drawing of a horse and rider attacked by a lion in the upper right-hand corner. This suggests that Rubens was rapidly noting down an idea as inspiration struck him, which he then developed into the central image of the composition.

The sketch is important as an example of a type of dynamic composition that became characteristic of Rubens, in which, to quote Jacob Burckhardt, "the richest symmetrical manipulation of a number of elements of equal value, of equivalents in the picture, is combined with a most animated, or even agitated incident to produce an effect which triumphantly captivates both eye and mind." A sense of symmetry and of unified composition is achieved by a balance of such "equivalents," which can be a light mass set against a dark mass, a series of curves or shapes set against counter-curves or shapes, even movement set against repose. These "equivalents" interpenetrate on a number of levels and

extend also to the emotional content, as here, where the fear of horse and rider is set against the ferocious savagery of the lion. Burckhardt suggested that this complex combination of unity and movement arose from a kind of initial vision in which the artist saw "at one and the same time a restful symmetrical arrangement of the masses in space and vehement physical movement." Certainly the inspiration for the overall composition came from Leonardo's lost *Battle of Anghiari,* known to Rubens from a copy, which was similarly dynamically conceived. Also, while an idea of the overall composition was clearly conceived of *in toto*, the details of the group seem to have been developed around the central image of horse, rider and lion, by setting the left-hand rider with the lance against it (he did not allow himself sufficient room to include the whole of the horse) and then sketching in the other balancing groups.

The technique is very simple: the chalk-white background is still visible beneath the broad, striated under-painting. The vertical and horizontal brushstrokes were applied with a coarse-bristled brush, which adds a lively broken texture to the overall design and provides a muted middle tone. The figural elements were then drawn in in outline with raw umber, set off with brown wash and highlighted with white. A touch of red ocher by the central horse's shoulder provides the only other color.

Such oil-sketches were valued as collectable items even in Rubens' own day, as much for their intrinsic beauty as for the fact that they were undoubtedly "autograph," unlike many of his finished compositions. Today when "finish" is no longer regarded as a necessary requirement of aesthetic worth, such sketches often seem to convey the passionate urgency and virtuosity of the artist even more brilliantly than the finished oil.

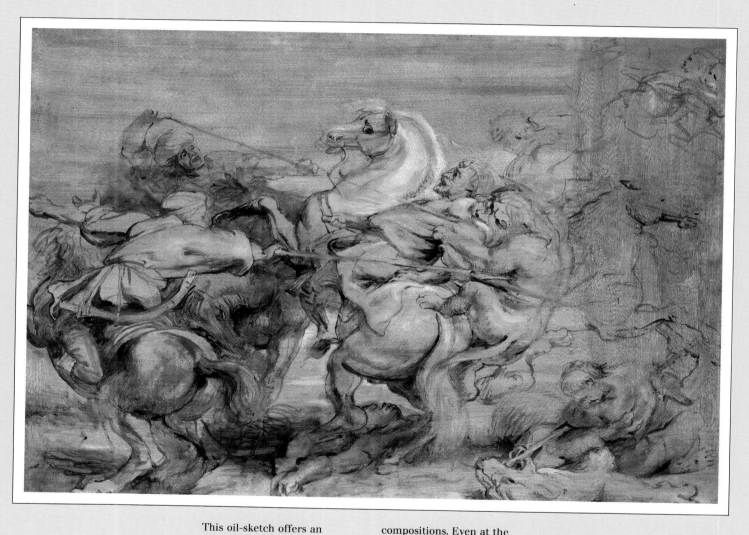

This oil-sketch offers an interesting insight into Rubens' technique and methods of working. Unlike the highly finished *modelli*, such as that for *Descent from the Cross* (see page 35), which would have provided studio assistants with a guide for the laying out of the finished painting, this monochromatic work is the equivalent of a preliminary tonal or linear sketch made to explore different ideas and compositions. Even at the early stages of planning a painting, Rubens preferred to work on a wooden panel rather than drawing on paper, and he used the same white background covered with a thin, striated underpainting as he used for his finished works. This type of dynamic composition, originally inspired by Leonardo's lost painting, the *Battle of Anghiari*, became a characteristic of Rubens' work.

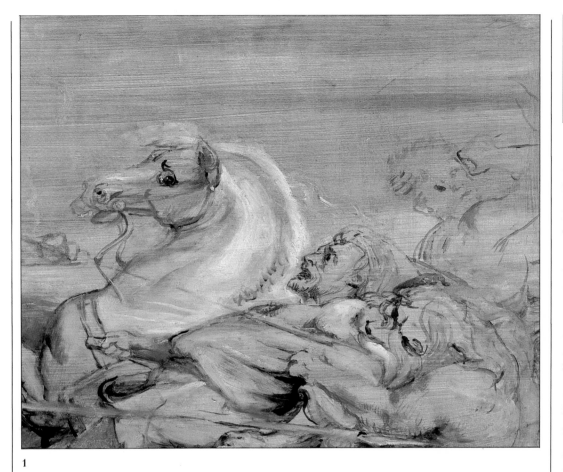

1

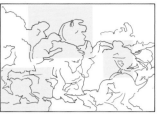

1 This detail shows the dynamic quality of Rubens' graphic work. The contours of horse and rider are sketched in with broken lines of uneven density and width. They swell and taper, conveying a sense of the urgency with which they have been drawn, which in turn gives a feeling of movement and energy to the horse. The heavy, solid forms of the neck are indicated by a simple broad white highlight, with streaks of white at the lower neck describing the mane.

2 This detail shows the earliest stage in the process of building up a design. The figures of the man and lion are roughly sketched in, with the main lines of force, of tension and opposition, established in terms of linear relationships. Subsequent applications of color merely serve to flesh these out with additional balancing elements of tone and hue, but great skill is required at this stage or the vitality established in the early stages could be lost or damaged.

3 *Actual size detail* This detail demonstrates Rubens' lightness of touch and restraint in the exclusion of unnecessary details — the complex figure is reduced to the expression of a single action. The apparent speed with which the figure has been drawn and the spontaneous, sketch-like style become visual metaphors for the energy and drama of the imagery.

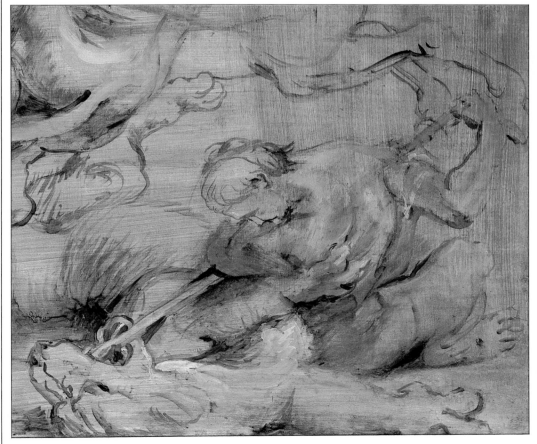

2

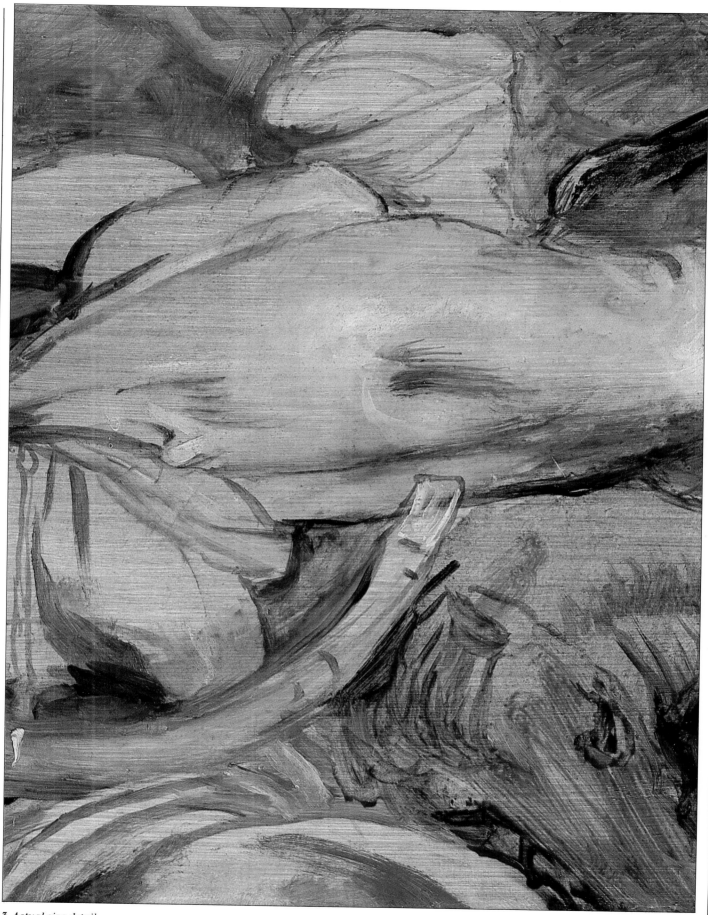

3 *Actual size detail*

THE ARRIVAL OF MARIE DE' MEDICI AT MARSEILLES

1622-26
155×115¼in/394×293cm
Oil on canvas
Louvre, Paris

This vast work was one of twenty-one canvases that Rubens executed between 1622 and 1625 to decorate a long gallery in the Palais du Luxembourg, the new home of Marie de' Medici, widow of the assassinated king Henry IV and ex-regent to her son Louis XIII. Louis had come of age in 1614, quarreled with his mother and banished her from Paris for several years. She was allowed to return only in 1620, and occupied herself, in her new role as Queen Mother, in decorating her new residence. She wished to be seen as a patron of the arts, as her illustrious ancestors had been In commissioning Rubens to paint, as the contract states, her "heroic deeds," her intention was to provide, not only a sumptuous decorative scheme in the great tradition of palace decoration, but also a monumental pictorial justification of her life that managed to suppress the more ignominious aspects of her career. Indeed the choice of subjects, although carefully and diplomatically drawn up by Rubens, was ultimately determined by Marie de' Medici herself, who had the final power of sanction or veto over certain scenes. A projected scene of "The Flight from Paris," for example, was replaced by the innocuous and more general "Felicity of the Regency."

The scene depicting her arrival at Marseilles on November 3, 1600, provided no such problems. It shows the landing of the young queen in France, shortly after her proxy marriage to Henry IV (which Rubens had witnessed in Florence). Rubens has infused the scene with allegorical personifications and mythological figures to glorify the event. The new queen is greeted by a figure representing France, in helmet and fleurs de lys, as well as another figure personifying the City of Marseilles, in a crown made up of towers. Winged Fame flies overhead, heralding the event with a trumpet. In the foreground Neptune has assured her safe arrival, and Triton and three muscular nereids moor the elaborately carved hull to land. The spectator can be in no doubt as to the special nature of the event. The epic treatment of the subject together with the monumental handling of the forms, the richness of coloring and the beauty of detail combine to give an impression of energetic adulation and extreme magnificence.

It was stipulated in the contract that Rubens himself was to paint all the figures, and though he relied a good deal on the help of assistants for background work and the laying out of the designs, it is clear that the major parts of this work are his own. Particularly spectacular is the treatment of the nereids and of the waves in the lower right foreground, which particularly struck the great nineteenth-century painter Eugène Delacroix. In an entry in his *Journal* for June 1849, Delacroix wrote, "I thought the nereids seemed more beautiful than ever. Only complete freedom and the greatest audacity can produce such impressions on me." He made a copy of one of them and took his assistant, Andrieu, to study the iridescent color of the flying drops of water. In another part of the *Journal* he writes that Rubens "...for all his...unwieldly forms, achieves a most powerful ideal. Strength, vehemence and brilliance absolve him from the claims of grace and charm." Delacroix recognized and admired the highly original use of the female nude, unusual in the history of art, to express not only sensuality but a generalized sense of rampant energy conveyed as much by the vigor of the brushstrokes as by the twisting forms themselves. Flesh becomes the vehicle for the expression of energy, and thus transcends ordinary eroticism.

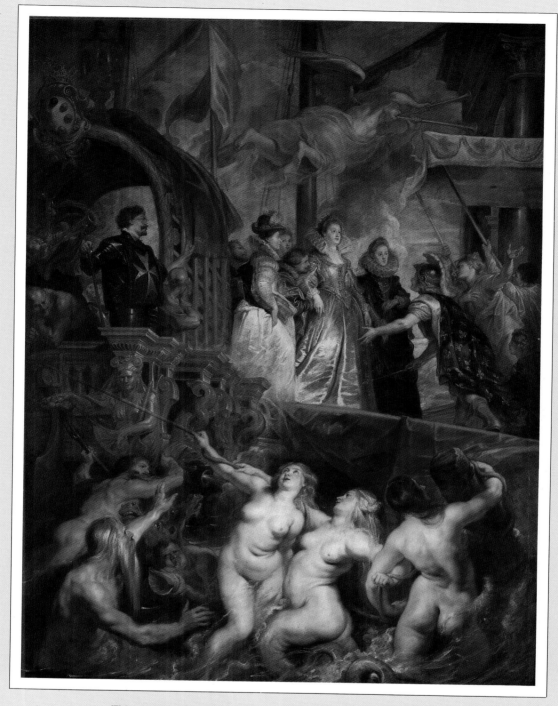

This painting, one of the twenty-one huge canvases that Rubens was commissioned to paint for Marie de' Medici's Luxembourg Palace, reflect his political role as arbiter of kings and princely propagandist. The works took three years to complete, and although Rubens' contract stipulated that he should paint all the figures himself, assistants were used extensively for background work and general laying out. The handling of paint is masterly, and shows Rubens' ability to render different surfaces with unfaltering sureness of touch.

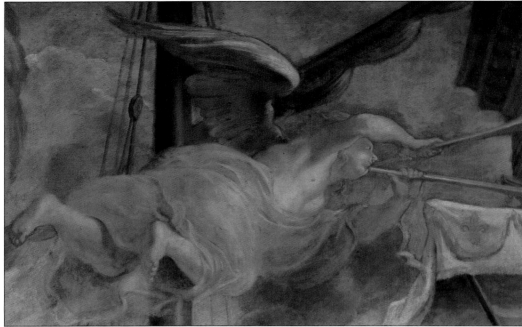

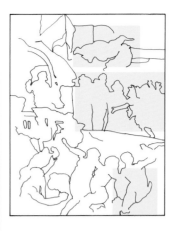

1

1 The winged victory is painted in dull colors in order not to disturb the formal prominence of the group of figures below. The limbs and drapery have been described in the most economical way, with highlights thickly applied in dry impasto.

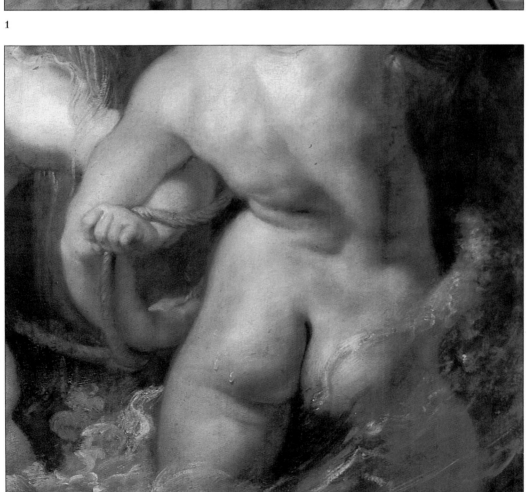

2

2 This detail shows Rubens' amazing facility with his medium, not only in the flesh but also in the way he has translated the effect of the turbulent water into paint. This has been built up in a dull and dilute blue-gray over the medium-brown underpaint, with thin washes of white applied on top in streaks that mimic the movement of the water. The effects of spray have been marvelously achieved on top of this, using thick, rather dry strokes of white smeared on with a broad brush. The drops of water on the buttocks are rendered by the simplest of optical means — points of white impasto and a thin brown glaze to indicate the shadows they cast.

3 The stunning surface treatment seen in such passages as Marie de' Medici's dress show the quality of the brilliant final touches Rubens was accustomed to bestow on these large-scale works drawn up largely by assistants. It is difficult to ascertain the degree of studio participation, but there may be a slight difference in quality between the face of the dowager queen and those of her attendants on the left.

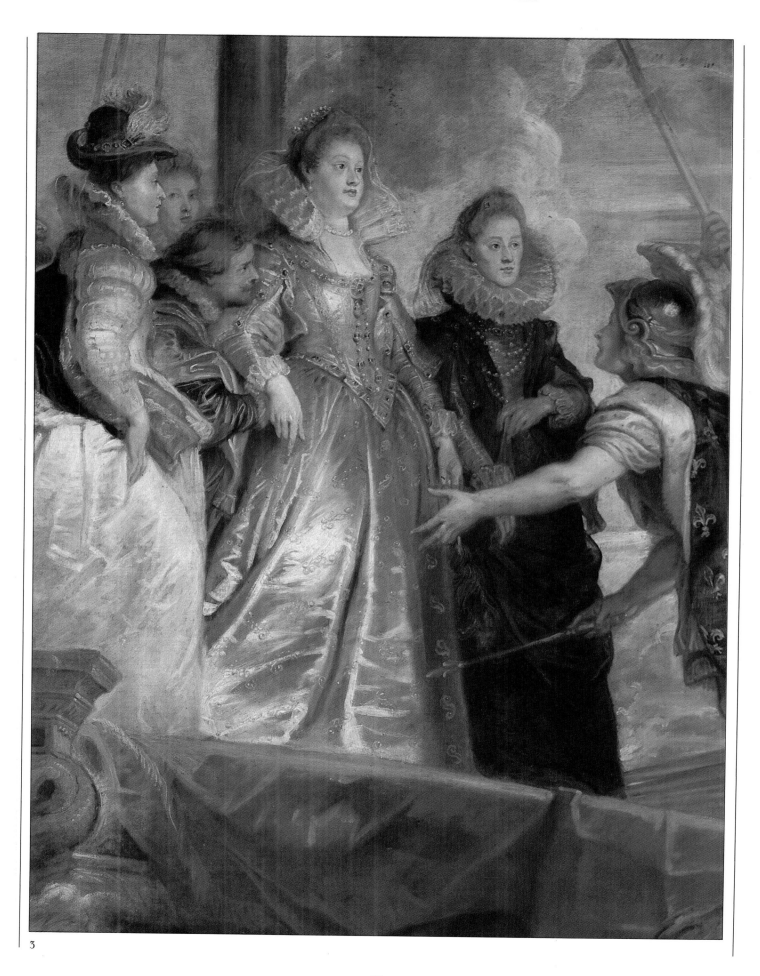

3

THE DUKE OF BUCKINGHAM CONDUCTED TO THE TEMPLE OF VIRTUS

c1625-7
25in/63.5cm square
Oil on panel
National Gallery, London

This small, brilliant oil-sketch is a preparatory work for a ceiling decoration, completed by 1627 for George Villiers, the 1st Duke of Buckingham, political advisor to Charles I of England. The finished ceiling, made for York House, the Duke's London mansion, was destroyed by fire in 1949.

Rubens first met Buckingham in Paris in 1625 when he was putting the final touches to the Marie de' Medici cycle. In the next two years he sold several paintings to the Duke, as well as the major part of his sculpture collection. Buckingham, as Rubens recognized, was an incompetent and unreliable diplomat, mistrusted abroad and unpopular at home. Rubens wrote of him: "When I consider the caprice and arrogance of Buckingham I pity the young king who, through false counsel, is needlessly throwing himself and his kingdom into such extremity. For anyone can start a war when he wishes, but he cannot so easily end it." In fact the duke was assassinated in 1628. Nonetheless Rubens apparently saw no contradiction in glorifying the virtues of the Duke in the grand monumental manner of Baroque ceiling painting. The notion of a figure being conducted heavenwards by attendant allegorical personifications originated in the church ceilings of Rome, where the figure was usually Christ or a saint. In taking over this device Rubens transforms the duke into something of a secular deity.

Rubens' mastery of allegorical storytelling is matched by his complete grasp of Baroque dynamic composition. Unlike the *Lion Hunt modello* (see page 39), this represents a stage further in conception. For here the colors are fairly clearly mapped out, though the changes that have occurred in working up the sketch, obvious in the various *pentimenti* (places where the paint has worn thin, showing underpainting), show that it was not the working *modello* on which the actual full-scale painting was based.

Rubens uses differences in strength of color and tone to rationalize the space and organization of the composition. The central group is treated with the strongest accents, not only in the strongest colors — the red and black of the Duke and the yellow of Minerva's cloak — but also with the strongest contrasts of tone, which provide an appropriate focus for the eye. The paint is also thickest in this part. The three Graces on the lower left are smoothly painted to a considerable degree of finish, but executed in paler tones. The contrast of light flesh tone and the surrounding light blue clouds is also less dramatic. The palest colors and area of least tonal contrast is reserved for the columns and the figures of Abundance and Virtus. This system of diminishing tones and increasingly pale coloring is used to convey a sense of the distances between the groups, but also on a more general pictorial level to create a central focus and to provide greater legibility, allowing the eye to pass more easily from group to group.

The painting is in general very thin. The priming is clearly visible, particularly at the edges, indeed it stops short of the top left and right corners, perhaps indicating that a smaller painted surface was at first intended. The dark umber outlines are also very visible, particularly in the marvelously freely drawn *putti* at the top, and accompanied by a brown wash in the lion and the figure of Envy. A *putto* just above the lion has been suppressed by white overpaint, but can still be clearly made out.

The colors that Rubens employed in his oil-sketches are generally duller than those of his finished paintings, and obviously it would have been wasteful to use expensive pigments on workshop *modelli*. It is probable that he used a dull red ocher color rather than the expensive crimson lakes or vermilions that are used in his finished pieces. Nonetheless one can see in a sketch of this kind Rubens' instinctive surety of touch and brilliance and speed of execution.

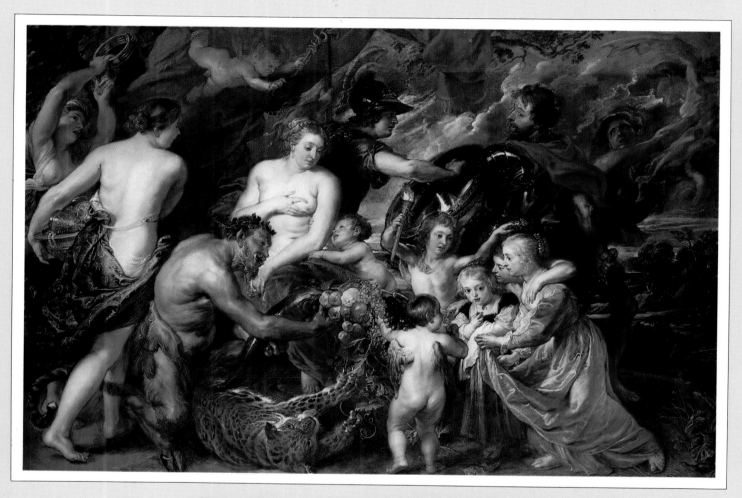

This sumptuous work, painted during Rubens' stay in England, was a presentation gift to Charles I in honor of his role as a peacemaker, and its subject is the appropriate one of the benefits of peace under threat of war. Unusually for Rubens, it is painted on canvas, not on a wooden panel, and the underpainting is darker than his normal one. It provides a wonderful example of his mature style, which by this time had loosened considerably and become more painterly, with less of the hard outlines and sculptural modeling of form that had characterized his earlier work. Once again, much attention has been paid to the skillful evocation of different textures and materials, seen for instance in the marvelously suggestive painting of the bowl of fruit, the leopard's fur and the polished steel of Mars' shield and armor.

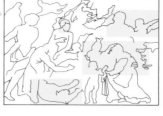

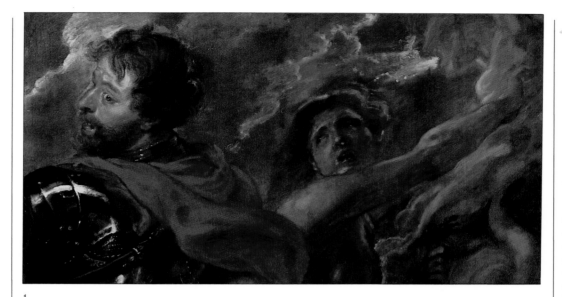

1

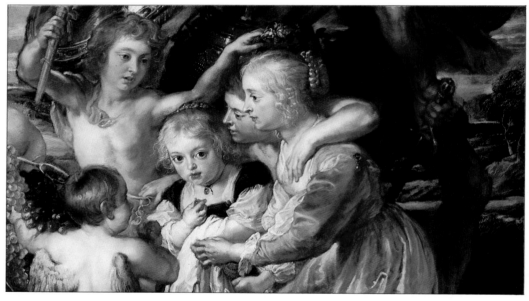

2

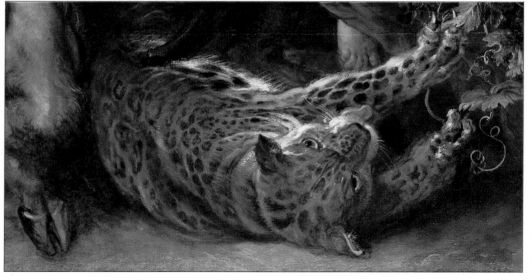

3

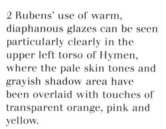

1 The head of Mars and a fury emerge only dimly from the dark brown underpaint, representing perhaps the least "finished" part of the painting. The effects of light reflected in the armor are created by working broad areas of black onto the brown underlayer, which stands as the middle tone between this and the brilliant streaks of white impasto, tinged at the ends with blue and a yellowish brown.

2 Rubens' use of warm, diaphanous glazes can be seen particularly clearly in the upper left torso of Hymen, where the pale skin tones and grayish shadow area have been overlaid with touches of transparent orange, pink and yellow.

3 The forms of the leopard have been built up very broadly, with yellow tones laid thinly on top of rough strokes of burnt umber and the spots painted in in thin dabs of dark brown and then glazed over ·with a modifying layer of yellow-brown varnish. Definition and a sense of texture have been given by thick strokes of impasted white tinged with yellow, and some touches of greenish blue.

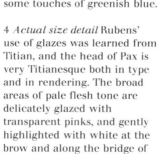

4 *Actual size detail* Rubens' use of glazes was learned from Titian, and the head of Pax is very Titianesque both in type and in rendering. The broad areas of pale flesh tone are delicately glazed with transparent pinks, and gently highlighted with white at the brow and along the bridge of the nose.

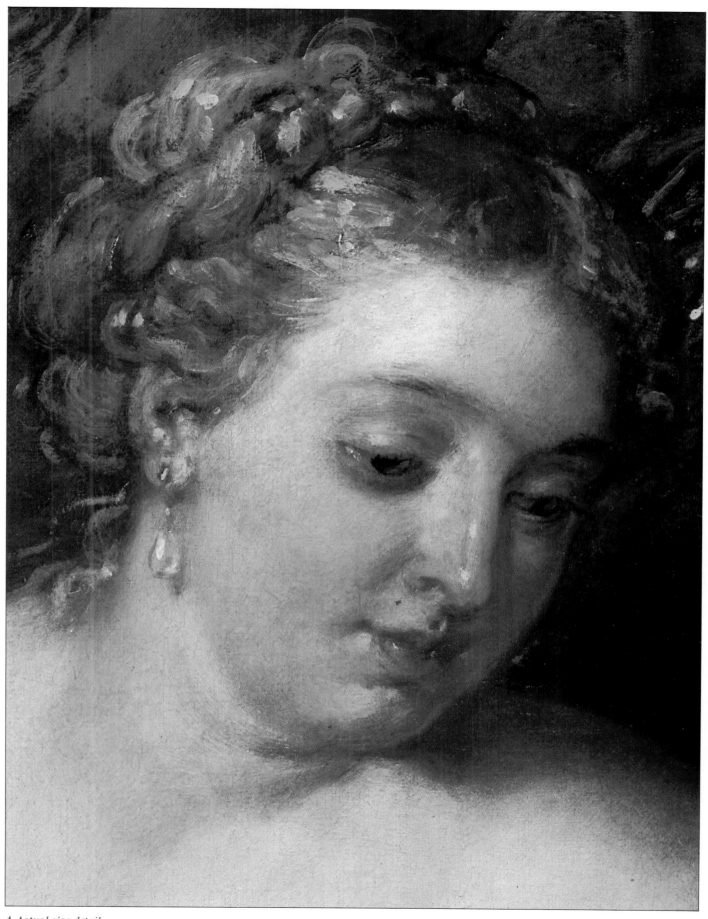

4 Actual size detail

THE RAPE OF THE SABINE WOMEN

c1634

66¾×93in/169.9×236.2cm

Oil on panel

National Gallery, London

The original purpose and location of this work remain unknown, although it was probably in the collection of Cardinal Richelieu in 1676. However, it is dateable on stylistic grounds to around 1634, and represents a fine example of Rubens' late style, particularly his ability to organize a huge number of figures into a satisfying whole.

The scene illustrates the famous episode in early Roman history, described by Plutarch, in which Romulus, in a ruse to increase the population of Rome, invited the Sabines, a tribe living near Rome, to attend some games, during which he ordered his soldiers to carry off a number of the unmarried women. The Sabines then attacked the Romans but were defeated. The Sabine women in the meantime accepted their lot, the population of Rome was duly increased, and peace was made with the Sabine tribe. Thus the story is not one of brutal violence: as Plutarch put it, the Romans "did not commit this rape wantonly, but with a design purely of forming alliance with their neighbors by the greatest and surest bonds." Although Rubens did not follow Plutarch literally on all points of storytelling, the painting follows the spirit of the literary account fairly closely. The women on the left-hand side are being carried off, having been separated from their menfolk, while behind, the Sabines rally to their defense, held off by Roman troops. The Roman soldiers in the foreground are setting about their task of abduction with the attitudes and expressions of noble and dutiful heroes rather than of lascivious seducers.

Formally, the composition is arranged into two dynamic masses held in precarious balance by the central foreground group and stabilized by the background architecture. Color and tonal arrangement are used in such a way that they clarify the narrative and unify the composition. The brightest point of the whole picture is the white flesh of the Sabine woman's exposed breasts in the center foreground, while the darkest is her deep blue drapery. This creates the area of greatest contrast of both color and tone, and provides an immediate focus for the eye, which is further strengthened by the strong modeling and close attention to descriptive details. The women in the left middle ground are treated in paler and more subdued colors, and the paint is thinner, without the plastic force of the foreground group. The background elements are paler still, with the colors even more washed out, the walls of the round vaulted building and the soldiers being just sketched in with very thin paint. This reduction in the intensity of the colors has been used more for reasons of pictorial unity than to indicate recession — according to the theories of aerial perspective, the distances implied by the relative sizes of the figures would not have been sufficient to merit such contrasts of tone and color. The "artificial" lightness of the background in fact has the opposite effect, of pushing it closer to the foreground, and the light area also provides a balancing contrast to the generally dark tonality of the foreground. This is an excellent example of Rubens' unique concern with unity and balance in all aspects of the composition, which was quite independent of conventional modes of perception or rules of perspective representation.

The handling of paint is breathtaking in its variety and suggestiveness of touch: for example the extreme thinness of paint in the figure of Romulus, who is drawn in with no more than a wash; the streaks of thick white impasto on the drapery of the central Sabine woman's shoulder; or the suggestion of a moving sword-blade in the fist of the left-hand soldier, evoked by the roughest smear of dry white paint over an undefined muddy brown ground. Despite attacks of gout, Rubens was still at the height of his powers.

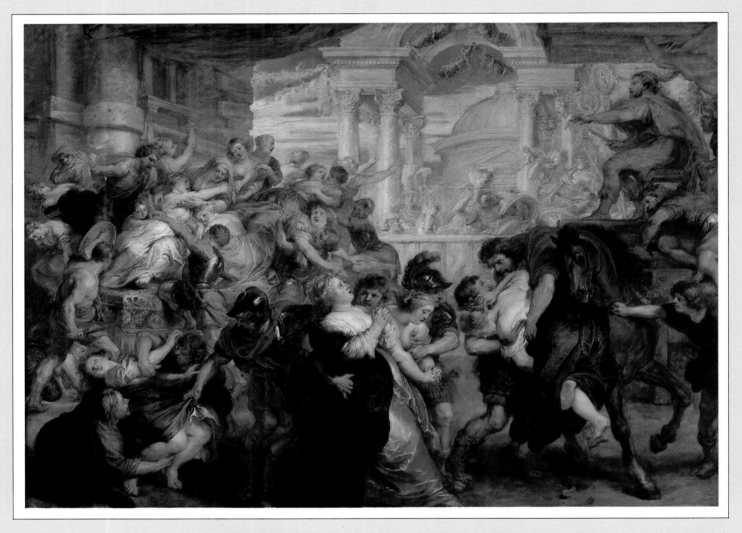

This is a particularly fine example of Rubens' late style, demonstrating both his expressive handling of paint and his ability to organize a large number of figures into a balanced but dynamic composition. Though increasingly hampered by attacks of gout, he had lost none of his brilliance of touch, and the variety and suggestiveness of the paint handling is breathtaking. Equally impressive is the way color and tone have been used to clarify the narrative as well as to unify the composition, for example the brightest point and area of greatest contrast is the Sabine in the center foreground, providing an immediate focus for the eye.

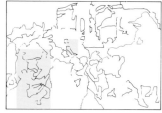

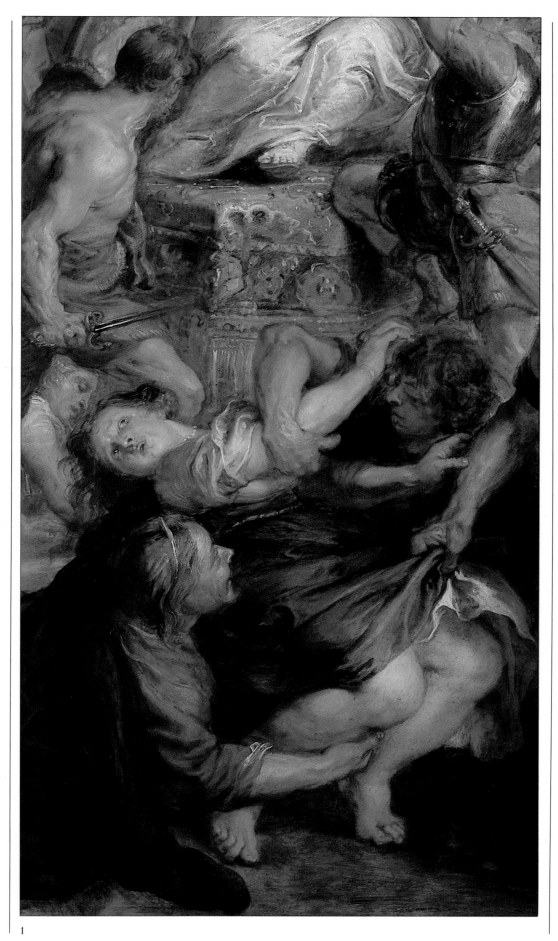

1 This detail shows a considerable range of colors employed in a relatively small space as well as illustrating the suggestiveness of Rubens' late style. The muscled arms and hands have been drawn in burnt umber and then vigorously brushed over in rich, thickly applied flesh tones, while the "white" drapery around the girl's upper arm is painted in a neutral green-gray repeated in the hair and arm of the old woman. This balances the brilliance of the central group. The girl's face is thinly painted, with touches of white impasto delicately suggesting tears in the eyes, and the blue dress is made up of a diaphanous dark brown layer over which rough strokes of black and blue articulate the folds.

2 *Actual size detail* The face of the Sabine woman in the middle ground is painted in paler colors and without the degree of definition given to those in the foreground group. Nonetheless, the feeling of her distress is clearly conveyed through Rubens' characteristic economy of drawing, demonstrating his ability to convey an emotion or expression in a brief "thumbnail sketch."

1

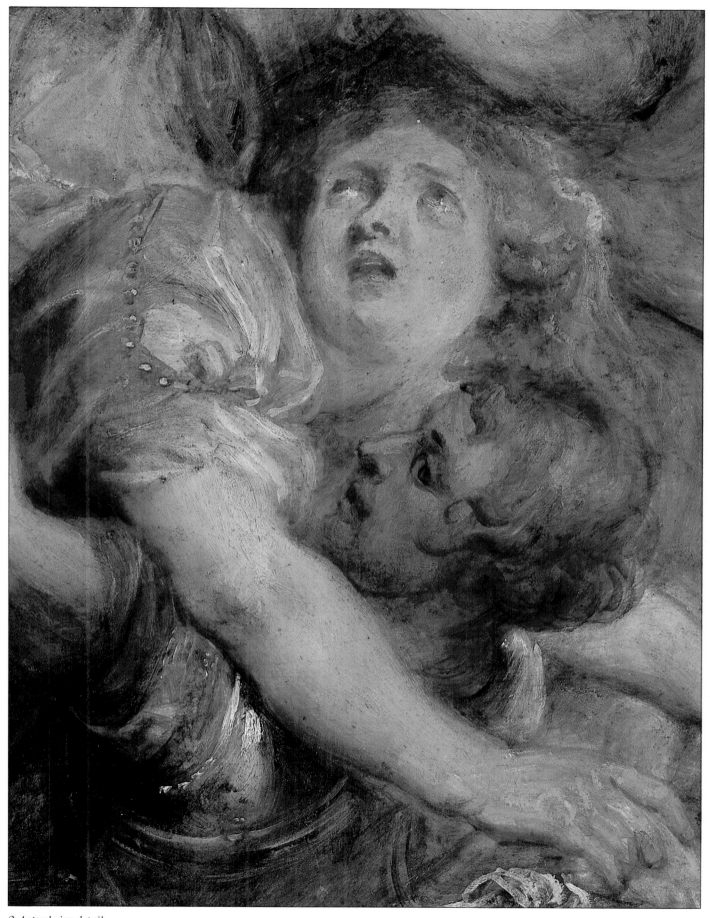

2 Actual size detail

Autumn Landscape with a View of Het Steen

c1636

52×90½in/132×230cm

Oil on panel

National Gallery, London

Rubens painted relatively few landscapes in the course of his career, but they were most frequent in the last decade of his life. Though initially trained in the studio of a landscape specialist, Tobias Verhaecht, he clearly aspired in his early career to the more exalted status of "history painter." Indeed he often collaborated with landscape specialists like his friend Jan Brueghel the Elder, executing the figurative elements against a landscape background by another hand. What landscapes he did paint were done "informally," as it were, springing from his own interest rather than being constrained by the demands or tastes of patrons. His approach to landscape is thus very personal, and shows little awareness of, or interest in, his contemporaries the great Dutch landscape painters.

Autumn Landscape was painted in all probability in 1636, Rubens' first year of residence in his new country mansion. He bought the Château of Steen, visible on the left side of the painting, together with a sizeable estate, as a suitable country retreat, "rather far from the city of Antwerp and off the main roads," as he himself wrote. The property brought with it a title, that of Lord of Steen, which he evidently valued — he is thus named in the epitaph on his tomb.

The painting depicts the estate in early morning, with a farmer and his wife on their way to market and a hunter stalking some early prey. The house and copse are bathed in a sharp, horizontal dawn light. Just as the space in his figurative paintings is defined by the figures that fill it, so in this landscape the sense of space is dependent on the physical objects — bushes, shrubs, trees, buildings and so on — that lead the eye from point to point into the horizon. It is a fundamentally concrete conception of space — the complete antithesis of the large, empty spaces of sky and distance typical of the works of such Dutch contemporaries as van Goyen or Salomon van Ruisdael — and in this case it

results in a slight lack of overall coherence.

The apparent evolution of the paintings seems to confirm this judgement. The support is made up of an astonishing seventeen panels that can be divided into three separate groups, suggesting (though by no means proving) that there were three stages of evolution. Beginning with the house, Rubens then seems to have extended the support to take in the landscape, and finally enlarged the whole composition by additional strips attached to top and bottom. *Pentimenti*, visible under X-ray, tend to confirm this view.

As with other landscapes by Rubens, it is not a true topographical reflection. The figure of the huntsman, the partridges, the magpies in the sky and the general layout of the composition are all derived from an engraving after Stradanus entitled "Duck Hunting." Moreover he has placed Het Steen in gently rolling countryside, whereas the land around it was in reality insistently flat.

The condition of the painting is generally good, though some passages of paint, especially around the wheel of the cart and the horses' legs, appear to be worn. The small figures close to the castle are not very characteristic of Rubens and may be later additions. The surface vibrates with color and movement, leading the eye in all directions to fresh pockets of interest. Rubens endows his plant forms with the same underlying energy that motivates his history paintings. The range of brushstrokes and the varied manipulations of paint are extraordinary — from the portrayal of the distant view, which was drawn in over the light ground in an extremely thin dark wash, and subsequently glazed over with greens and yellows — to the thick scumbles of dry paint that brilliantly suggest the tangle of blackberry bush and undergrowth; or the free strokes of smeared white impasto that evoke the reflected light on the tree trunks. This ability to suggest form by means of raw oil paint is equal to that of the late Rembrandt.

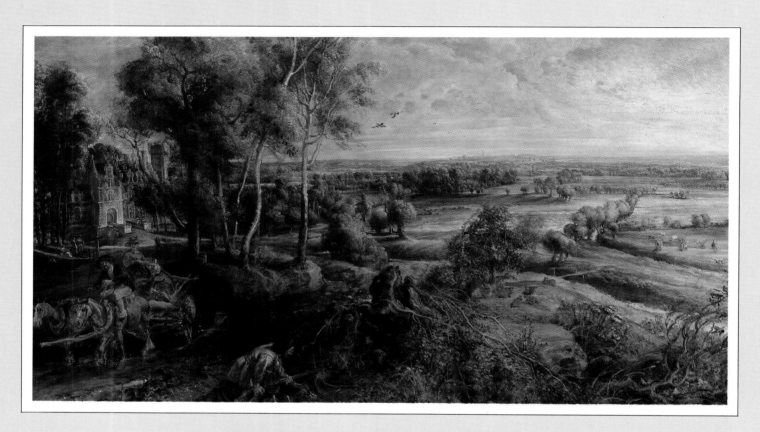

Although Rubens had trained in the studio of a landscape painter, Tobias Verhaecht, he painted relatively few landscapes himself, and in some of his works he would execute the figural elements while another artist painted the landscape background. However, he began to be more interested in landscape when he bought the Château of Steen as a country retreat in 1636. Now less constrained by the demands of patrons, he was free to explore more personal and private subjects. This work depicts the countryside around his new residence, which can be seen on the left-hand side, but like his other landscapes, it is not a true topographical representation. The general layout and some elements, such as the figure of the huntsman, are derived from an engraving of a duck hunt, and the countryside is shown as gently rolling while in fact it was quite flat.

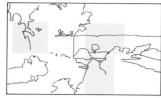

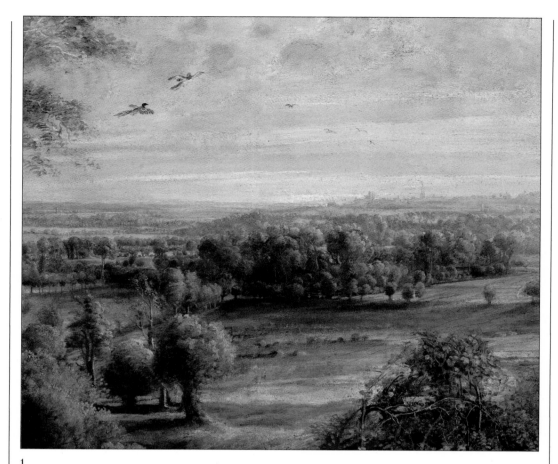

1

1 The distant landscape has been created by drawing the details of buildings, woodlands and shadowed hills in very dilute paint and then overlaying the drawing with successive layers of equally thin pale greens and yellows. Final touches were the small thick strokes of yellow to indicate the patches of sunlight.

2 The chateau, bathed in the sharp, angled light of early morning, is very thinly painted, the main walls mapped out by a glaze of green ocher and the detailing defined by dabs and touches of yellow and white impasto. Tiny drops of pure white impasto serve as the reflections of light in the glass windows.

3 The tangle of trees and undergrowth is one of the most thrilling passages in the painting. It is brilliantly worked up in a series of muddy greens, yellows, orange-browns and earth reds, all seemingly haphazardly imposed onto a loosely indicated network of tendrils and branches. The shadowed areas have been glazed over in dark brown, with definition provided by wedges of an orange hue, thickly applied. Viewed at close quarters, these streaks and dabs lose their identity as forms, but when seen from a distance they immediately become recognizable.

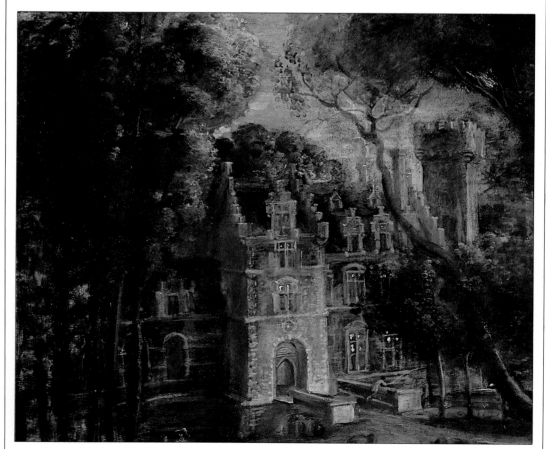

2

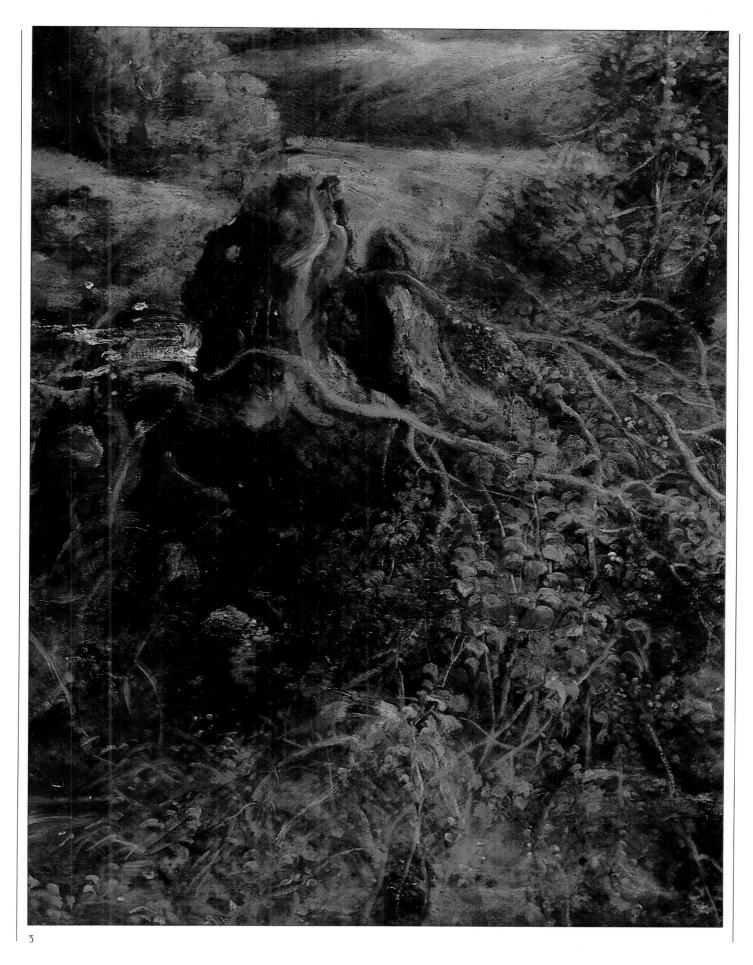

3

INDEX

Page numbers in *italic* refer to illustrations and captions

A

Adoration of the Kings, 13
Albert, Archduke of
    Austria, 13
allegory, 46, *47,* 50
Allegory of Peace and War,
    16, 22, *50-3*
Anne of Saxony, 7
Antwerp, 8, 13
The Arrival of Marie de'
    Medici at Marseilles, 42-5
The Artist and his Wife in a
    Honeysuckle Bower, 26-9
assistants, Rubens' use of,
    14, 16, 39, 42, *43, 44, 45*
Autumn Landscape with a
    View of Het Steen, 15, 20,
    58-61

B

Baroque, 46, *47*
"Belvedere torso," *11,* 22
Brant, Isabella, 13, 26
Breugel, Jan the Elder, 58
brushstrokes, 15, *15,* 19, 34,
    42, *48*
    drapery, 30, *32, 35*
Buckingham, First Duke of,
    (George Villiers), 46
Burckhardt, Jacob, 38

C

canvas, 27, 50, *51*
Caravaggio, Michelangelo
    Merisi da, 11, *13*
    Death of the Virgin, 11
    The Entombment, 11, *13*
Carleton, Sir Dudley, 14
Catholicism, 6, 8, 34, *35*
ceiling decorations, 6, 11,
    11, 19, 46, *47*

classical influence, 6, 8, *11,*
    14, 22, *31*
classical subjects, 19, 22,
    50, 54
color, *46,* 54, *55, 56*
    brilliant, 19
    broad washes, *24*
    browns, *32,* 34, *36*
    deceptive, *33*
    harsh, *7,* 8, 22, *23, 24*
    Italianate, 22
    muted, 26, *32,* 38, *44*
    oil sketches, 46
    range, 22, *24,* 30, *46, 56*
    rich, 30, 42, 50
    to clarify narrative, *55*
composition, *15,* 19, *23,* 34,
    38, *39, 48,* 54, *55*

D

Delacroix, Eugène, 42
The Descent from the Cross,
    14, *20,* 30, *34-7, 39*
detail, *7, 26,* 30, *41,* 42
diplomacy, and Rubens, 11,
    14-16, *43,* 50
disegno, 6
drapery, 30, *32, 35*
drawings, 9, 27
The Duke of Buckingham
    Conducted to the Temple
    of Virtus, 20, *46-9*
Dürer, Albrecht, 8

E

The Entombment, 12, 13
eroticism, *16, 17,* 19, *31,* 42

F

faces, *32, 36, 37*
family portraits, 19
figure painting, 34, 36

Flemish influence, 22, *24,*
    26
    see also Mannerism
flesh-painting technique, 8,
    22, *24, 25,* 26, *28,* 30, *32,*
    34, *36,* 46, *53,* 54, *56*
Fourment, Helena, 16, 19
Fourment, Susanna, *15*
Francken, Frans the
    Younger, 30

G

glazes, 30, *36, 44,* 52, *52, 53,*
    60
graphic work, *40*
ground, 15, *15,* 30, *36,* 38, *39*
Guild of Arquebusiers, 30,
    34, *35*

H

Helena Fourment and her
    Children, 18, 19
Helena Fourment as Venus,
    16, 17, 19
Het Pelsken, 16, 17, 19
Holbein, Hans, *Dance of*
    Death, 8
hunting scenes, 38

I

Ignudo, 8
impasto, *28,* 30, 34, *44,* 50,
    52, 56, 58, *60*
Isabella Brant, 27
Italian influence, 8, 9, 22,
    23, 31

J

The Judgement of Paris, 8,
    9, *22-5*

L

landscape, 19, *24*, 58, *59*
Laocoön, 11, *11*, 14, 34
Leonardo da Vinci,
    Battle of Anghiari, 38, *39*
light, *7, 13, 28, 48, 52, 60*
Ligne-Arenberg, Margaret
    de, 8
Lion Hunt, 35, 38-41;
    (detail), *15*
Lion and Tiger Hunt, 38

M

Mannerism, 6, *7,* 8, 22, *23*
Mantua, 9
marriage portraits, 26
Medici, Marie de', 9, 16, 42
Michelangelo, *8, 9, 31*
    Ignudi, 9, 9, 10, 11
    Leda and the Swan, 31
modello, 15, 15, 30, 34, *35,*
    38
monarchy, 6
movement, 19
musculature, *8,* 11, 22, *31,*
    34, *36, 58*

N

nature, and Rubens, 6
Noort, Adam van, 8
nudes, *9,* 42

O

oil-sketches *see* sketches

P

panel-painting, 30
    see also wooden panels
peasant types,

Caravaggio, *13*
Philip III, King of Spain, 11
Piles, Roger de, 11, 14
Plutarch, 8
portraits, *6,* 19, 26
Presentation in the Temple,
    34, *35*
priming, 15, 30, 34, *35,* 46

R

Raimondi, Marcantonio, 8,
    22, *23*
    The Judgement of Paris, 23
The Rape of the Sabine
    Women, 19, *54-7;*
    (detail), *15*
Raphael, 8, 11, 13
    The Judgement of Paris,
    22, *23*
realism, Caravaggio, *13*
religion, 6, 7
Rembrandt, 19, 58
Rickox, Nicholas, 30
Royal Bounty Overcoming
    Avarice (sketch for), *10*
Rubens, Jan, 7-8
Rubens, Peter Paul,
    artistic training, 8
    as collector, 13-14
    as court painter, 9-13
    as diplomat, 11, 14-16, 50
    early life, 7-8
    influences on, 11, 19, 22,
    31, 35, 50
    marriage, 13, 26
    working methods, 14

S

Samson and Delilah, 30-3,
    34; detail, *15*
sculpture, influence on
    Rubens, 14, 22, 34, *35*

scumbling, 15, *29,* 58
self-portraits, *6,* 19
Self-portrait (detail), *6*
Seneca, 8
sketches, 9, *10,* 11, *13,* 15,
    30, 38, *39*
Spain, 11-13
Sperling, Otto, 14
statuary *see* sculpture
Stoics, 8
Stradamus, 58

T

texture, 26, *27, 32, 36, 43, 51,*
    52
Tintoretto, Jacopo, 11
    Minerva and Mars, 50
Titian, 11, 13, *16, 17,* 19, 50,
    52
    Ecco Homo, 50
    Girl in a Fur Wrap, 17, 19
    Worship of Venus, 50
turpentine, to dilute paint,
    15

U

underpainting, *15,* 26, *28,*
    39, 50

V W

Van Dyck, Sir Anthony, 14
Veen, Otto van (Octavius
    Vaenius), 8
Verdonck, Rombout, 8
Verhaecht, Tobias, 8, *59*
Vincenzo I Gonzago, Duke
    of Mantua, 9, 11
Visitation, 34, *35*
water, *44*
Whitehall, Banqueting Hall
    ceiling, *6,* 11, *11,* 19

William of Orange-Nassau,
    7
wooden panels, as painting
    support, 15, *15,* 30, 38, *39,*
    58
Wtewael, Joachim, *The*
    Judgement of Paris, 7, 8

Art-Dutch

Art-Dutch